T0375169

GOD'S PATH
TO
DISEASE-FREE
LIVING

What the
Scriptures
Tell us About
HEALTH

Bob McCauley, ND

WESTBOW
PRESS®
A DIVISION OF THOMAS NELSON
& ZONDERVAN

Copyright © 2017 Bob McCauley, ND.

All rights reserved. No part of this book may be used or reproduced by any means, graphic, electronic, or mechanical, including photocopying, recording, taping or by any information storage retrieval system without the written permission of the author except in the case of brief quotations embodied in critical articles and reviews.

Scriptures taken from the Holy Bible, New International Version®, NIV®. Copyright © 1973, 1978, 1984, 2011 by Biblica, Inc.™ Used by permission of Zondervan. All rights reserved worldwide. www.zondervan.com The "NIV" and "New International Version" are trademarks registered in the United States Patent and Trademark Office by Biblica, Inc.™

This book is a work of non-fiction. Unless otherwise noted, the author and the publisher make no explicit guarantees as to the accuracy of the information contained in this book and in some cases, names of people and places have been altered to protect their privacy.

WestBow Press books may be ordered through booksellers or by contacting:

WestBow Press
A Division of Thomas Nelson & Zondervan
1663 Liberty Drive
Bloomington, IN 47403
www.westbowpress.com
1 (866) 928-1240

Because of the dynamic nature of the Internet, any web addresses or links contained in this book may have changed since publication and may no longer be valid. The views expressed in this work are solely those of the author and do not necessarily reflect the views of the publisher, and the publisher hereby disclaims any responsibility for them.

Any people depicted in stock imagery provided by Thinkstock are models, and such images are being used for illustrative purposes only. Certain stock imagery © Thinkstock.

ISBN: 978-1-5127-6593-9 (sc)
ISBN: 978-1-5127-6595-3 (hc)
ISBN: 978-1-5127-6594-6 (e)

Library of Congress Control Number: 2016919519

Print information available on the last page.

WestBow Press rev. date: 04/03/2017

I dedicate this book to my Lord Jesus Christ, who has taught me everything about life and health.

I want to acknowledge that Jesus is a Westernized version of Yeshua, which is Aramaic for Joshua. Our Lord's full name was Yeshua Ha Mashiach, meaning "The Anointed One". Jehova is a Westernized version of Yahweh, which refers to God the Father. In this book, I will use Jesus for the name of Our Lord, The Anointed One.

Health books require medical disclaimers because if you don't provide them, you become liable in every way. I don't have any problem stating that I know almost nothing about medicine. But then, what does it take to understand how to achieve great health: a doctorate or a few letters behind your name? I am a certified nutritional consultant, a certified master herbalist, and a naturopathic doctor, which took me a total of eight years to complete. I have learned a lot by reading and talking to others about health. although most of what I know about health has come to me through experience and intuition. However, medical and legal disclaimers are necessary, so here is mine.

The purpose of this book is to educate. It is sold with the understanding that the publisher and the author shall have neither liability nor responsibility for any injury caused or alleged to be caused by the information contained in this book. This book is not intended in any way to serve as a replacement for professional medical advice. Rather, it is meant to demonstrate that aging can be slowed and even reversed and that great health is achieved when the most fundamental nutritional needs of the human body are met. This book is not meant to diagnose anyone of any disease. If you feel the need, always consult a doctor or another medical professional when you have an illness or disease of any kind. I admit to knowing little if anything about medicine and therefore would never offer medical advice to anyone for any reason. The author offers health advice that is his personal opinion only.

The United States FDA has not reviewed ionized water, *spirulina*, *chlorella*, angstrom minerals, or living (raw) foods and therefore has made no determinations or assessments about it.

It is hereby declared that the Ninth and Tenth Amendments to the US Constitution and those rights so granted to Americans by them fully apply to this book.[1]

Note: Alkaline Ionized Water and other key terms are italicized in this book for emphasis.

Contents

Author's Introduction

To one there is given through the Spirit a message of wisdom, to another a message of knowledge by means of the same Spirit, to another faith by the same Spirit, to another gifts of healing by that one Spirit. (1 Corinthians 12:8–9 NIV)

I consider my primary profession to be that of a teacher. Education is my vocation, and its reception constantly teeters on my abilities as a communicator. I communicate best through the written word. I present to you here what I understand about health as it relates to the temple of God, our bodies, in the simplest, easiest-to-understand format I can communicate it to you. My intent is always to educate my readers about true health, the kind of health that most people only dream about and that only God can possibly provide us with. I consider the health protocol I promote not as opinion but as the truth about health and nothing less. It advocates nature in its purest form, which only God is capable of creating. God became flesh (John 1:14), a man known as Jesus Christ. Just as Jesus honored His temple, we should honor ours.

Because to this you were called so that you may inherit a blessing. (1 Peter 3:9 NIV)

Those of you who are familiar with the Bible will perhaps find that some of the passages I refer to in this book are taken out of context. It may appear that way because I am attempting to introduce a new concept that most Christians have never heard of. While the traditional interpretations of these Bible passages may temporarily be put aside here, it does not mean that I intend to dispense with them completely. Rather, I am attempting to demonstrate that the Bible may be viewed and understood from a perspective that stands apart from traditional interpretation. Viewing the Bible through this prism will help you to understand my seemingly radical health protocol. Therefore, I ask your understanding and indulgence regarding my unorthodox interpretation of certain Bible verses.

In short, this book is my interpretation of the Bible as it relates to health. However, I am not alone. Many others know and believe what I know and believe about health. I count myself among the chosen whom God has blessed with this knowledge of health and the understanding of how we can honor our temple. This is the path to disease-free living. After reading this, I pray you will also find yourself among those who have decided to follow this message of wisdom, knowledge, healing, and faith so you may obtain true health.

Preface

(A Must Read)

The mystery that has been kept hidden for ages and generations, but is now disclosed to the Lord's people. (Colossians 1:26 NIV)

You cannot understand this book if you don't read this preface. I almost subtitled this book *A Christian Health Revolution* because it is a truly revolutionary way to view health and how we ought to view the temples, our bodies, that God has given us. The ideas in this book will change your view of how health is actually obtained. It will challenge your understanding of your body and your obligation to honor it. It will cause you to waken your obligation to honor one of God's most precise gifts, your body. Whether you are Christian or not, you will never think of yourself, your life, and your body in the same way after reading this book.

The health protocol explained in this book is the next revolution in Christianity. This revolution concerns the recognition that the temple of God is within us because our bodies literally are temples of God. And they are far more important temples than one built of wood, steel, and brick.

Do not feel that I am either accusing or ridiculing you about your present lifestyle and eating habits. On the contrary, this book is meant to encourage you to become aware of what God wants for us. If you desire to be among those God calls His followers, then adopting this health protocol even to the slightest degree will help bring you closer to God. That I promise you.

This book will challenge your concepts of what foods we should consume if we want to be healthy. It is an empowering message of hope and triumph over disease. It will confront your presuppositions about what causes disease and why disease never just happens to us but is always a result of the choices we have made. You will learn that the body becomes full of disease when we put the wrong substances into it; therefore, disease is exclusively a result of our diet. You will be compelled to examine why you eat the foods you consume each and every day of your life. After reading this book, perhaps you will conclude that the medical establishment has not sanctioned it, so it must not be true. But if you read it with an open mind, you will be faced with an internal struggle, a war within, because you will know that you are putting the wrong foods into your body, things that lead to disease, and that you must change a fundamental aspect of your life in order to truly honor the temple God has given you.

I grew up on the standard American diet (the SAD), which is comprised mostly of cooked and processed foods. When it came to health, I listened to the endlessly changing lists of foods that were thought to be healthy or unhealthy. Coffee and chocolate were found to be harmful one day then to have antioxidant properties the next. Margarine was determined to be healthier than butter, and then a few months later we were informed it was much worse. Many people naturally become skeptical, if not dismissive, when such conflicting information was constantly being released by the media. We've all seen the news magazine covers that declare everything we believe about a particular aspect of disease or medication has been found to be completely wrong and therefore "the mystery remains" about what is healthy and what causes certain diseases in some people and not in others. Without a consistent message, it's easy to become discouraged and lose interest in anything, including health. Like almost everyone else, I lived in a state of complete ignorance about what is actually healthy because I let the media and the medical establishment dictate my beliefs about health.

The consensus among the general population is that health is more a matter of opinion and conjecture than actual fact. What is healthy for one person isn't necessarily healthy for another. Justification for these false beliefs is founded upon faulty interpretation of facts, such as who gets cancer and who doesn't. While certain foods may agree or disagree with different people, the reasons why we get sick with arthritis, fibromyalgia, diabetes, or cancer depends on our bodies' ability to fight those diseases and the environment we create within ourselves that either encourages or discourages disease. It has nothing to do with randomness or family history.

In the past, I found hope in the new drugs that were constantly being developed that would cure me of the diseases I was inevitably going to get. I believed that my family genes were responsible for the diseases I was prone to and would one day likely get. I would become frightened to learn another family member had contracted cancer or some other disease. I wrongly believed that I was fair game for the same disease since the probability of which diseases we get arrives with us at birth in our genes. Heart disease "runs in my family," and I believed there was a good chance I would fall victim to it. I believed that because I'd been taught all my life that health was elusive, a guessing game where the actual truth about health would never be determined. We constantly hear that the cure for terrible diseases such as cancer is "right around the corner." In short, I believed in the medical establishment. I believed in man. I believed that science would eventually find a cure for all our diseases. However, finding a cure to the medical industry doesn't actually mean *discovering* a cure. Rather, it means inventing a cure, and man will never invent cures to the wrath of diseases we are prone to.

When I discovered the truth about health ten years ago, it was as though scales fell from my eyes the way they did from the apostle Paul's when the Lord revealed Himself to him. Now I no longer live in the darkness of ignorance. I have stepped into the light and know the truth about what leads to health and what actually causes disease. I will never return to that life of ignorance. I have been blessed to learn this knowledge, and I wish to impart it to you in the pages that follow. The one thing I can personally assure you of is that if you adopt this lifestyle, you will feel great each and every day, perhaps better than you have ever felt in your life. I can personally testify to the greatness and power of its results.

I hope the blunt, straightforward writing style of this book does not interfere with its powerful message. I present this to you with the greatest understanding and compassion. In some ways, this message may appear harsh and extreme because it is contrary to everything you have learned about health and diet. That aside, I have tried to write this with the compassion that is expected of Christians and that which was taught to us by our Lord, Jesus Christ. The road to true health is hard, but I will be with you as a whisper of encouragement every step of the way, both in spirit and in prayer.

The wrong diet results in filling the body with nearly every disease known, and only a natural diet can put the body in a position where it can perform a miracle and heal itself of any disease. Science will *never* find a cure for *any* disease. Science has developed vaccinations for bacterial and viral diseases, but it has yet to invent a cure for them. I will never again put my faith in humankind and what science believes it can achieve. Instead, I have learned to put my faith in God only and the great health He graces us with when we follow His rules and honor the temple He has blessed us with.

Chapter 1

The Temple of God Biblically Defined

> Therefore honor God with your bodies. (1 Corinthians 6:20)

> The God who made the world and everything in it is the Lord of heaven and earth and does not live in temples built by hands. (Acts 17:24 NIV)

At the mention of a church or temple, we first picture a brick, stone, or wooden structure built by men and machines. The image of soaring steeples, stained glass, and religious statues comes to mind. It is the place where we worship God together. However, a far more important temple is the temple that God gave us at birth—our bodies.

> And in Him you too are being built together to become a dwelling in which God lives by his Spirit. (Ephesians 2:22 NIV)

When we stop to consider which is the greater temple, a community church or the human body, it is easy to recognize that the body is a glorious work of God[2] and a church is a simple human-made structure.

The human body is comprised of an average of ninety trillion cells. We must be humble and know that science still understands little about God's miraculous creation called the human body. It is arrogant, boastful, or perhaps naive to think that we will ever know all there is to know about it. Every bodily system, organ, and cell exists to perform a specific task. The more we learn about the human body and how it functions, the more we are awed by its complexity, functionality, and cellular interdependence. It was once thought that each cell in the body operated independently from the others, but in recent years researchers have discovered that cells are constantly communicating with one another throughout the body, and the breakdown of that communication is one of the first signs of disease. The more we study the enormously intricate mechanisms of the human body, the most complex organism known, the more evident it becomes that only divine involvement could have possibly created it. It is full of order and deliberate design, and where there is a design, there must be a designer behind it.

Jesus's Declaration of the Body as a Temple

> What agreement is there between the temple of God and idols? For we are the temple of the living God. (2 Corinthians 6:16 NIV)

Stating that His body was the temple of God was another part of Jesus's revolution against the world and all it stands for. After Jesus cleared the temple of the moneychangers, He was confronted by the Jews, who asked Him by what authority He did so.

> Jesus answered them, "Destroy this temple. I will raise it up again in three days." (John 2:19 NIV)

The Jews scoffed at Him because they thought Jesus was referring to the Holy Temple where they worshiped each day.

> But the temple he had spoken of was his body. (John
> 2:21 NIV)

Jesus's declaration that the body is the temple of God went far beyond the Pharisees' worldly perspective of God and what our relationship with Him should be. The Pharisees never accepted the fact that the body is the temple of God, in part because it would have lessened their public status. Their livelihood depended on the holy temple in Jerusalem and the money it brought in, which was a main contribution to their social and professional status. The Pharisees were worldly in nature and loved material possessions. Their power was of the world; therefore they turned a deaf ear to the revelation of truth that Jesus preached.

We Admire or Detest Our Bodies—We Do Not Honor Them

> Do nothing out of selfish ambition or vain conceit,
> but in humility consider others better than yourselves.
> (Philippians 2:3 NIV)

Most people look in the mirror and either approve or disapprove of the way their bodies look. They think their bodies should look sexy and appealing. Others look upon their bodies with disappointment and self-loathing. Some see themselves as hideous sacks of drooping flab. Many have tried every diet known or joined a gym in their quest for health and beauty. Since nothing has worked, they are ready to give up because they know in their hearts that they still are not healthy after all their efforts. As people get older, they often begin to lose their will to change, rationalizing that it's too late in life for them to do anything about it.

The body we see in the mirror should not be regarded merely as a thing of beauty or loathing, because what we are looking at is not only our body but God's temple. Looking at it that way, we will either be satisfied or dissatisfied with it. We should be satisfied that we have honored our temple when it is healthy and strong because it means we have followed God's simple rules for properly maintaining His temple. We should be proud of ourselves. We should admire our accomplishment in the eyes of the Lord, but we should not be haughty or arrogant about how good we look because that is vanity. God creates beauty in each of us, and it is our responsibility to discover that bounty within.

When we are dissatisfied with how our bodies look, we should understand it is because we have not honored our temples by eating the right foods and exercising. We have not maintained our temples according to God's principles of health. Therefore, we have no one to blame except ourselves when we are sick with disease because we are the ones who have not followed the health protocols intrinsic in nature, which is created by God and therefore is a reflection of Him as are we.

Most people associate aging with deterioration, which they wrongly assume is inevitable. This kind of thinking excuses laziness and lack of determination to live up to the high standards that God has set for us regarding our temples. They are not easy, but His standards never are. They are not for the weak of spirit, but His standards never are. We can always make excuses as to why we don't measure up to the standards He sets for us. God's way is difficult and rocky. It is never the easy path, but it is the right path. It is meant to be that way, for we are meant to struggle. God's way is arduous, but the rewards of fidelity following it are immense, for in them is a great gift—that of complete freedom and contentment. When you are healthy and your health is rooted in God's law, you have a physical foundation that a meaningful spiritual life can be built upon. When you are sick with disease but have a meaningful spiritual life, you have a spiritual foundation that great health can be built upon.

It takes tremendous discipline to always put the right foods into our bodies. That is why we must rely on more than just discipline. We must ask for God's assistance in giving us the strength to resist and the courage to change. It is difficult to be humble. It is even more difficult to completely surrender ourselves to God's will and His desire for us to honor and keep the temple He has graciously made us clean, fit, and strong. This is the path to disease-free living.

A story that illustrates the power and necessity of humility is one about a renowned abbot of a monastery long ago. The abbot could not understand the meaning of a particular passage in the Bible, so he prayed and fasted every day to understand its meaning. After one month he became disappointed and angry because he still did not understand it. He bowed his head in defeat and asked for mercy. He left his tiny room, vowing to ask the first monk he saw if he knew the meaning of the passage. If he did not know, the abbot would stop the next monk he found and ask the same until he had asked everyone in the immense monastery, no matter how new or seasoned they were. As he started down the hall, an angel appeared and stopped him. "Your one moment of genuine humility is worth so much more than all your prayer and fasting," the angel said and then revealed the meaning of the Bible passage to the abbot.

We must also be humble and accept what God wants for our temples so they can function to capacity. We glorify God when our temples shine brilliantly and are disease-free because we have followed God's health protocol. When we do this, the light of God not only shines on us but also from within us. Others will be drawn to it and want to possess the light themselves because it is the unmistakable signature of God.

Our Duty to Honor the Temple of God

> Do you not know that your body is a temple of the Holy
> Spirit, who is in you, whom you have received from
> God? You are not your own; you were bought at a price.
> Therefore honor God with your bodies. (1 Corinthians
> 6:19–20 NIV)

We are under the false impression that health is complex and therefore must be beyond our grasp. Many of us believe we are eating healthily when in fact we are not. Faux health is feeling good while living with the knowledge that you are declining and that it is only a matter of time before disease invades your body. Health is simple to understand, but it is not easy to follow. Health is so simple that anyone can understand it. We don't need to know anything more about health than what substances we should consume and which ones we should not consume, what does and does not belong in the body. Our bodies know what to do with the nutrients we consume. However, it does not know what to do with substances that do not belong in it. Once we have learned this, we then have a difficult choice to make. This is the reason why it is important to start our children out on the only diet that leads to true health.

> He gives strength to the weary and increases the power
> of the weak. (Isaiah 40:29 NIV)

We must control our appetite for the foods and tastes we crave and have become accustomed to eating over many years. We must not do this for ourselves but for God and the glorification of His temples, our bodies.

In order to truly succeed and honor our temples, we must choose to surrender to God's will for us. We must be *selfless* to accomplish this because we can never be selfish with God and expect to have a meaningful, proper relationship with Him. Our relationship with God should be progressive and ever-expanding. Each day we should strive to know Him better, and this is only accomplished through His word, prayer, meditation, reading scripture, service, and work. For a believer, a day spent earnestly working is a day spent with God. The environment for that is best created when we live in the *now*, the present moment and when we live in a way that does not invite disease.

> Therefore do not worry about tomorrow, for tomorrow will worry about itself. Each day has enough trouble of its own. (Matthew 6:34 NIV)

Live in the moment, for what you *can* be today, not what you *might* be tomorrow. When we live in the *now* and not for yesterday or tomorrow, we face an immediate choice of health or disease, which is determined by what we put in our bodies. Accumulated "tomorrows" produce empty yesterdays. To say that you have become the victim of disease is true only in that you have become prey to the dietary choices you have made. Our choices should never be about us but rather about God and His will for us. As Christians, we typically try to find time to fit God into our busy schedules. Instead, our days should be built around God. The same should be true of our diet. We should consider what is best for our temple and build our health around that rather than what we like the taste of and what we are accustomed to eating. Like all that God demands of us, this is a more difficult but rewarding path.

A man reaps what he sows. (Galatians 6:7 NIV)

Hearing about this health protocol of natural foods and clean alkaline water and then following through with that message can be compared to the Parable of the Sower (Matthew 13:3–9). A farmer scattered seed one day. Some fell along the path and were eaten by birds. Some fell on rocky places, where it sprang up then died because the soil was shallow and the sun withered it. Others fell among thorns, where they were choked. Some fell on good soil, where it grew strong and multiplied.

Where will the seed of hearing about true health fall in your life? Will you not listen at all because your heart is hardened to God's message of true health? Will you listen to this word of health, get excited, and then go back to your comfortable lifestyle of foods that please your taste buds yet lead to chronic disease? Will you wilt under the pressures of friends and family to eat the way everyone else does because if you don't eat that way you will be socially ostracized? Or will you shun the world, follow God's path to true health, and prosper in your enhanced relationship with Him?

A great challenge you will face when following God's health protocol is changing the social aspects of your lifestyle to fit what God requires of us if we wish to be healthy. However, it is no different from changing your life to follow God in any other way. For instance, when we first discover God, we are immediately confronted with either changing our sinful ways or remaining sinful, to stay with God or turn our backs on Him.

Jesus was a revolutionary. However, He was not a political revolutionary. Rather, He was a true revolutionary in the sense He revolted against the world, its ways, and every convention. He had a greater impact on the world than anyone who has ever lived, whether you believe He was the Son of God or not.

> Whoever finds his life will lose it, and whoever loses
> his life for my sake will find it. (Matthew 10:39 NIV)

If we deny our true selves, we will lose our spiritual lives. This means that we cannot go on sinning, doing that which is shameful, and expect to have a meaningful relationship with God. We also cannot desire to truly honor God but not honor the temple He has given us. If we dishonor our temple, we dishonor God. If our temple is full of toxins and pollutants, it is a result of our diet and habits, which is solely our responsibility. We are obligated to clean it since we have created a mess inside ourselves that invites disease. We must clean our temple by changing our diet and the lifestyle that created our unhealthy situation.

If you hear the word of true health that honors His temple, will you be like the rich man who wanted eternal life, but wouldn't give up his wealth because of his attachment and addiction to it? (See Matthew 19:16–23, the rich man and the kingdom of God.) If we want desperately to follow God, we should end our attachments and addictions to the foods we love. This will take time. Changes such as those are difficult because they form much of the foundation of our everyday lives. Our parents and grandparents often gave us the recipes for the foods we eat every day of our lives. Unfortunately, they are most often for cooked foods that lead to disease of every kind.

As Christians who want sincerely to honor God's temple, we must start new traditions of health to replace the old traditions that lead to disease. Our gatherings, which often revolve around food, must offer the foods and beverages that honor the temple of God by keeping it clean and bringing it great health. When we are pleasant yet firm in our resolve to eat only healthy foods, others will take notice and follow us. It is incumbent upon Christians to set the example of how God expects us to act and lead our lives, including what we should eat.

Flowing With Nature: The Three Kings of Health

We refer to the result of God's creative life force as nature. To prevent and heal the body of any disease, we only need to do three things: *Hydrate*, **A**lkalize, and **D**etoxify *the Body*. These are the *Three Kings* that must rule our health, which I will explain in detail in this book. God invented everything that exists, including nature. Since nature was created by God, it is a reflection of God. The further we get from nature, the further we get from God. When we flow with nature, we are a part of nature. Flowing with nature means that you are flowing with God's creation, which we rule over (Genesis 1:26). When unadulterated nature is flowing through your body, God's creation is flowing through you. God will never allow disease to come into His temple if it is kept clean and flowing with His unadulterated creation. We must fill our bodies, which are God's creations, with nature, which is also God's creation, if we wish to be healthy.

Disease Is Not a State of Victimhood

> The thief comes only to steal and kill and destroy; I have come that they may have life, and have it to the full. (John 10:10 NIV)

When we follow nature, we follow God. When we stray from nature through the wrong diet, the result is poor health. If we are sick, it means that we have strayed from nature, and we must get nature back into our lives if we wish to again be healthy. As we call God into our lives through prayer, so should we also call God into our lives through our diet so we may truly honor the temple He has given us. Having a clean temple clears our minds and enhances our spiritual lives because we are better able to realize and fully comprehend our relationship with God under those conditions.

Everyone wants to be healthy. No one wants to be sick or even admit they ever get sick. Sadly, most who hear this message of true health will remain sick because of their refusal to leave their old habits behind and start putting in their bodies the foods that naturally belong in them. God's temple can only be properly served and maintained by the living foods that are part of God's creation, that which we call *nature*. Only that which comes from nature will ever make us healthy. There is no substitute for nature because it the result of God's ever-moving hand. Everything man creates to make himself healthy will end in failure.

The Unclean Temple
The Result of the Wrong Diet is Disease

> You, however, are controlled not by the sinful nature but by the Spirit, if the Spirit of God lives in you. And if anyone does not have the Spirit of Christ, he does not belong to Christ. But if Christ is in you, your body is dead because of sin, yet your spirit is alive because of righteousness. (Romans 8:9–10 NIV)

If we create an acidic (low pH) environment in the body by years of consuming cooked foods and other acidic substances, such as drugs, alcohol, cigarettes, soft drinks, processed sugar, etc., then we become vulnerable to any disease that invades the body. The more acidic a person is, the more susceptible he or she becomes to disease. Disease is opportunistic, and as it flourishes in the body, it creates a more acidic environment in order to spread further until it consumes the entire body.

Disease is essentially a mechanism that nature uses to recycle something that is no longer a part of itself. All chronic disease is unnatural and a result of the wrong diet. It has nothing to do with genetics, as we are led to believe. Chronic disease destroys what is natural. Therefore, it is a result of unnatural circumstances. In this case, it is the result of the foods and liquids we naively consume. Chronic disease of any kind is never found in animals that live in the wild except for those that have been exposed to chemical toxins. Only bacterial and viral diseases are found in wild animals. If we begin to feed animals cooked and/or processed foods, it is only a matter a time before chronic disease of all kinds, including cancer, appears in them. Humans are the only species on earth that experience chronic disease other than the animals we domesticate and make our pets.

How We Destroy the Temples God Has Given Us

> If anyone destroys God's temple, God will destroy that person; for God's temple is sacred, and you together are that temple. (1 Corinthians 3:17 NIV)

There are foods that honor God's temple and foods that do not honor it. We would not throw trash inside the sanctuary where we worship, nor should we put things in our bodily temple that do not belong in it. We consume things that do not belong in the body because we like how they taste and we mistakenly believe they are good for us.

> For if you live according to the sinful nature, you will die; but if by the Spirit you put to death the misdeeds of the body, you will live. (Romans 8:13 NIV)

When we consume junk foods such as potato chips, donuts, soft drinks, snack cakes, etc., we are trashing our temple. These are poisonous substances, not foods, because they are completely void of nutrients, and we consume them exclusively for their taste. The offense against our temple is blatant and egregious. These are terrible addictions that must end if we want to truly honor the temple that God has given us.

We are raised as children to live on a diet that consists primarily of cooked and processed foods. Aside from our appearance, what we inherit from our parents and grandparents are dietary habits. And it is a lifestyle of cooked foods from which all chronic disease is derived. We are what we eat. More specifically, we are what our bodies assimilate. If we eat foods that destroy us from within, we are destroying ourselves with each bite we take. Therefore, we have only ourselves to blame for our demise. It is the slowest suicide known, with every victim unaware that they are not only destroying themselves but that all disease is reversible.

> All of us also lived among them at one time, gratifying
> the cravings of our sinful nature and following its desires
> and thoughts. (Ephesians 2:3 NIV)

The average person's diet is comprised of a variety of foods that do not belong in our body if we expect to be healthy. Our taste buds rule our lives and determine our fate. It is difficult to control the words that come out of our mouths. It is even more challenging to control our carnal urges. But it is most difficult to control what we put into our mouths. We eat the foods we eat because they stimulate our senses and therefore they please us. And because of this pleasure, we keep coming back for more, just like any other addiction. An addiction is when we repeatedly do something we know is bad for us, but we won't stop doing it. We have become accustomed to eating the same foods over many years. Some foods contain physically addictive substances, and others stimulate pleasurable chemical responses in the brain. Therefore, what rules our health is our taste buds and lifelong eating habits that we refuse to acknowledge as unhealthy. We have installed them as lord over our temple. We have made them the final determination over how healthy we actually will be and how we choose to honor our temple. For those who chose to live on a diet of mostly cooked foods, the result is always the same: disease of any and all kinds.

> Those controlled by the sinful nature cannot please God. (Romans 8:8 NIV)

When we consume substances that toxify our bodies, we are in fact defiling our own temples. It's as though we are walking upon the cleanest floor with dirty, muddy, greasy boots instead of clean sandals. The body is a living temple of God, not just flesh and bone that we own and therefore can treat any way we want to. On the contrary, we must remember that we are purchased at a price (1 Corinthians 6:19–20).

We must change our lives and take our first steps toward respecting what God has given us. With time, we will begin to realize that we have been dishonoring God's great gift to us, that of our temple. It is our duty as His children to keep it clean, strong, and shining from within.

> In the beginning, God created the heavens and the Earth. (Genesis 1:1 NIV)

God created us with these same attributes: those of heaven and earth, spirit and flesh. We are obligated to serve both aspects of His glorious creation. We honor God by not sinning and by caring for our flesh, our temple, through a natural diet of living foods that have not been diminished by cooking or processing. Living foods referred to in this book include raw fruits, vegetables, nuts and seeds, and fresh foods that are not cooked or processed in any way. Preferably, they are foods grown organically, without the use of herbicides or pesticides. However, I would rather eat a commercially grown raw food than an organically grown cooked food anytime.

The Signs of Disease: Acidity and Toxicity

If you are sick with any disease, you know two things about your temple and its state of health. First, you know that it has a deficit of electrons because your body is acidic. pH is a measurement of the concentration of positive and negative ions. When they are present in equal quantities, we have reached a state of equilibrium within the body and our pH will be 7.0. When your body has accumulated too many positively charged hydrogen ions, then you become acidic and your pH is low. An acid environment in the body encourages disease. Disease will not live in a body where the pH environment is in balance, which means it is close 7.0.

If you are sick with any disease, you also know that you are toxic because disease lives on toxins. In the absence of toxins, disease cannot exist in the body. If you are healthy, your body will not contain substances that do not belong in it. Anything that does not perform a useful function in the body should be regarded as a toxin that needs to be removed. The body, our temple, is only truly glorious when it is free of toxins. Toxins turn the body into a garbage hull. A temple free of toxins is a disease-free temple. Disease is a symptom of not honoring what God has given us. A diseased body is a testament to our transgressions against God's living temple.

The Temple Is Capable of Healing Itself of Any Disease

> Praise the Lord, my soul, and forget not all his benefits—
> who forgives all your sins and heals all your diseases.
> (Psalm 103:2–3 NIV)

God created our temple perfect in every way. While it is true that we all will someday die (Genesis 3:19), God did not create our temple to house disease. To say that disease is an inevitable part of life and that we all will succumb to it is to conclude that God's work is not perfect. It is a false assumption to think the body is a flawed vehicle designed to inevitably become filled with disease and die. One could only conclude from this theory that God Himself is imperfect because the design of His temple is imperfect. However, since God is perfect in every way, this simply cannot be true. If we are to assume that God is perfect, then His creation called our temple must also be perfect in every way, including its ability to cure itself of any disease. To say otherwise would be to suggest that God's abilities are limited when in fact they are boundless (Matthew 19:26).

How long we live is irrelevant. What is important is that we have quality of life today, which is tremendously enhanced when we honor God's temple. The only way we can obtain true health is by having a clean temple that is free of toxins. Curing the body of disease will only happen when we clean it thoroughly from within and without.

> But if they do not wash their clothes and bathe themselves,
> they will be held responsible. (Leviticus 17:16 NIV)

External hygiene, cleaning the outside of our temple on a daily basis, is extremely important if we expect to truly honor our temple. Those who don't bathe themselves daily create an unhealthy environment for their temple, further inviting disease. Caring for the body's largest organ, our skin, is incumbent upon every Christian. There is no excuse for a Christian not to look healthy, and the first thing anyone sees when they meet us is our skin. A person's illnesses are betrayed through their skin and eyes, which are immediate indications of someone's state of health. (See appendix 3.)

Health is a habit, not an event. It cannot be crammed for as though it were a college examination. If we wish to honor God, cleaning the outside of our temple is as important as cleaning the inside. These are habits we must develop, cultivate, and incorporate into our everyday lives.

I am the Lord, who heals you. (Exodus 15:26 NIV)

Like any machine, one must put the right substances in the body if we expect it to work correctly and not malfunction. When we stop putting the wrong things in our bodies and we start putting the right things in our bodies, the result is disease-free, healthy bodies. Putting the right substances in the body essentially chases out all diseases that are housed in it, which is a direct result of ingesting the many kinds of poisons that we unwittingly consider to be healthy foods.

With great determination, discipline, and inner strength disease can be overcome and completely reversed. It is the way God designed our bodies to work. Triumph over disease is essentially no different than triumph over sin because it is a triumph over temptation. It is never beyond our ability to be healthy any more than it is beyond our ability to stop ourselves from committing any other kind of sin. You may be tempted to cheat on your spouse. However, it is difficult to stay loyal to your spouse over many years. It is easy to steal, be selfish, be greedy, and commit other sins. It is difficult to remain loyal to God and follow His path into the light of truth, health, and cleanliness.

> But you are a chosen people, a royal priesthood, a holy
> nation, a people belonging to God, *t*hat you may declare
> the praises of Him who called you out of darkness into
> His wonderful light. (1 Peter 2:9 NIV)

The rewards of practicing God's laws, including His laws that honor our temple, are too innumerable to imagine. Doing so will take both your physical and spiritual life to a place few have ever visited, let alone conceived of. I have personally experienced a level of health I never knew existed before I began following this health protocol. I would be lying to say it is easy to maintain, but it is definitely worth it. I struggle every day, but my reward is often beyond words and simply a thing you have to experience for yourself to understand its joy.

I am crying to you about your health from the desert the way others have cried from lonely places wanting others to hear God's message. This is a difficult message to hear, but it is not beyond your reach. This message is tough love, but love nonetheless. We all face tremendous difficulties in our lives. Some we feel are impossible to overcome. But with God, everything is possible. God never gives us challenges that we cannot overcome because He is infinitely fair. As with all the challenges that confront us, all we need to do is turn ourselves toward the face of God and ask for His mercy, and it will be granted to us.

Chapter 2

Our Temple Requires Water

I baptize you with water for repentance. (Matthew 3:11 NIV)

Water is referred to 617 times in the Bible, making it the most prevalent substance mentioned in it. It's mentioned eleven times in the first chapter of Genesis, fifty-four times in the entire book. Water is the first element mentioned in the Bible (Genesis 1:2–6). God saved humanity through Noah when the world flooded. The Red Sea parted to save the Jewish people, then defeated their enemies during the Exodus. Moses got water from a rock during their forty years in the desert (Exodus 17:1–7). Water is mentioned fifty-three times in the Psalms alone. Bathing and water purification rituals are mentioned numerous times in both the Old and New Testaments. Jesus was baptized with water; Jesus's first miracle was to change water into wine, which was the commencement of His ministry. He performed several miracles on the Sea of Galilee, including walking upon water.

The prevalence of water in the Bible is no coincidence because water is the most important substance the body requires other than the air we breathe. Water is the cornerstone of health. It is a universal solvent and the body's lubricant. Proper hydration of the body is crucial to human health in countless ways. You will never be truly healthy if you are not sufficiently hydrated. When we begin making water a big part of our lifestyle, we take our first steps toward true health.

Every organ in the body heavily depends on water to function properly and to its capacity. We are mostly water. The average human body is 69 percent water. The brain is 85 percent water, bones 35 percent water, blood 83 percent water, and the liver 90 percent water. When we become dehydrated, we put our health in immediate jeopardy. Thus, we gamble with our lives without realizing the dangerous high-wire we are walking when we don't drink enough water.

We must drink half our body weight in ounces minimum each day. For instance, if you weigh 200 pounds (90 kg), you should consume 100 ounces (3 liters) of water each day. However, I recommend people drink a lot more because we lose that amount of water through the basic functions of the human body, those of urination, perspiration, respiration, and defecation.

Living Water

Never again will they thirst. (Revelation 7:16 NIV)

Alkaline *Ionized water* **has many aliases:** alkali water, alkaline water, alkalized water, cluster water, microcluster water, micro water, reduced water, miracle water, ion water, ionic water, electron water, hydroxyl water, electrolyzed water, living water.

Alkaline Ionized water is known by many names. Jesus is referred to as Living Water in the New Testament. Alkaline Ionized water is also often referred to as living water because ionization wakes up and enlivens conventional water that is considered sleeping or dead because it is of little good to the body other than to hydrate it. Alkaline Ionized Water goes far beyond that and is a world apart from conventional water.

If we wish to truly honor the temples God has given us and be healthy, we need only do three things: *Alkalize, Hydrate,* and *Detoxify the Body.* If we achieve this, we can prevent and even cure the body of any disease. Alkaline *Ionized Water* provides all these qualities and much more. It *Alkalizes, Hydrates,* and *Detoxifies* the body more effectively than any other substance. No other water can bring about these results. Running normal tap water through a water ionizer creates a miracle that can help put your body into a position of health you never imagined you could achieve.

Alkaline Ionized Water is not only the best water we can drink; it is the best substance we can possibly put in our body. Consumption of Alkaline Ionized Water is critical if we wish to bring the body into balance, a state known as *homeostasis.* Fresh and strong is the best way to drink Alkaline Ionized Water once you've become acclimated to it. How long that will take depends on your overall health and toxicity.

Alkaline Ionized Water is negatively charged and alive with electrons, which our bodies are starved for. Alkaline Ionized Water is a liquid antioxidant, which is why it can and should be considered the best substance we can put in the body. I have become biologically younger by drinking it, and you will too.

The Opposite of Ionized Water

Water cures, but purified water is a detriment to the health of anyone who consumes it. Purified water is produced by *deionization, distillation,* or *reverse osmosis* and should not be consumed for three reasons. It acidifies, leaches minerals from the body, and the large size and shape of its water molecule clusters do not hydrate the body well. In fact, long-term use of purified water can leave us dehydrated.

Alkaline Ionized Water and purified water are exactly the opposite from each other in every regard:

- Purified water is acidic. Alkaline Ionized Water is alkaline.
- Purified water does not effectively hydrate the body; Alkaline Ionized Water is extremely hydrating.
- Purified water leaches minerals from the body. Alkaline Ionized Water provides minerals to the body.[3]
- Purified water does not provide the body with oxygen. Alkaline Ionized Water provides the body with oxygen.
- Purified water does not scavenge for free radicals. Alkaline Ionized Water does scavenge for free radicals.
- Purified water encourages oxidation of the body. Alkaline Ionized Water reduces oxidation.
- Purified water has a positive ORP, which is an oxidant. Alkaline Ionized Water has a negative ORP, which is an antioxidant.

The Miracle of Ionized Water

Alkaline Ionized Water is by far the most superior drinking water available. The invention of the water ionizer is one of the great health breakthroughs of the twentieth century. Alkaline Ionized Water is electronically enhanced water created through electrolysis. It is produced by running normal tap water over positive (cathode) and negative (anode) electrodes, which ionizes the minerals in the water, creating positive (hydrogen) and negative (hydroxyl) ions. The electrodes are composed of titanium, the hardest metal known, and coated with platinum, which is an excellent and durable conductor.

The magic comes when a membrane separates the hydrogen and hydroxyl ions, creating alkaline and acidic water. These two waters are always produced simultaneously during the ionizing process, 70 percent Alkaline Ionized Water and 30 percent Acid Ionized Water. Therefore, producing one gallon of Alkaline Ionized Water yields approximately 0.7 gallons of alkaline water and 0.3 gallons of acid water.

To *ionize* means to gain or lose an electron. Essentially, the ionization process robs an electron from one molecule and donates, or transfers, it to another molecule. The other water produced during the ionization process contains molecules that have been robbed of an electron. These molecules are known as hydrogen ions (H+), and they are what make the water acidic, resulting in a low pH.

These yin/yang waters produced by ionization are the exact opposite from one another. Both Alkaline and Acid Ionized Water have extraordinary properties and benefits, although their respective uses could not be more different. We consume the Alkaline Ionized Water. The Acid Ionized Water should never be consumed. Alkaline and Acid Ionized Waters have a beneficial effect on everything it comes in contact with as long as it is used properly. Alkaline Ionized Water is one of the most significant preventative health advances of our generation because it is the most beneficial substance available to the human body.

Alkaline Ionized Water is an antioxidant that provides the body with an abundance of oxygen, which gives us energy. It possesses a negative charge, or ORP, which is also an antioxidant. It balances the body's pH, which helps prevent disease because it is alkaline. It is a powerful detoxifier and superior hydrator because of its small water molecule cluster size.

Antioxidant Qualities

The centerpiece of Alkaline Ionized Water are its antioxidant properties. It is truly miraculous that normal tap water can be instantly transformed into a strong antioxidant. Alkaline Ionized Water has two antioxidant qualities: its negative charge and the presence of hydroxyl ions. Water has a low atomic weight (18), and when ionized it becomes the most absorbable antioxidant known. The lighter an object, the more easily it can be absorbed by the body. Other antioxidants have a much higher molecular weight, which make them less easily absorbed by the body.

All liquids have an oxidation reduction potential (ORP), which is the millivoltage (mV), or vibration, it possesses. A negative ORP can reduce, or negate, oxidation. Strong Alkaline Ionized Water has an ORP of -50 mV to -450 mV, depending on the source water and how many minerals it contains. The more minerals in the source water, the stronger the Alkaline Ionized Water will be. This low negative number means that the water has a very high potential for reducing oxidation. A beverage that has an ORP of -350 mV is healthier to consume than -150 mV because it negates oxidation of the body more effectively. Therefore, the lower the ORP of the water, the greater potential it has to reverse the aging process of the body at a cellular level.

All fresh-squeezed vegetables and fruit juices have a negative ORP, which varies depending on which vegetables and fruits are juiced. Therefore, they are considered antioxidants because they reduce the potential for oxidation in the body. Conversely, if these juices are heated above 118° F, pasteurized or otherwise processed, the negative ORP antioxidant property is destroyed, and these same food have become oxidation agents that accelerate aging. In fact, all its rejuvenation properties have been removed, and now the food has been transformed into mere sustenance that provides the body with calories, almost no nutrition, and helps to acidify it. Enzymes must be present in a food for it to truly be considered a rejuvenating substance. This same principle is true for Alkaline Ionized Water. If it is heated, it will quickly lose its negative charge because the fragile, fleeting electrons will dissipate. Electrons are thousands of times lighter than protons, and thus they are more easily dispersed and scattered than protons. However, Alkaline Ionized Water's other properties such as alkalinity and reduced water molecule cluster size, remain intact to some degree for a longer period of time.

As a substance oxidizes, its ORP rises. Oxidation means to react with oxygen. Rust is metal that has been oxidized, which is an example of slow oxidization. Fire is an example of fast oxidation. In the human body, oxidation is caused, in part, by free radical damage. Unstable oxygen molecules rob us of electrons, which causes oxidation, leading to accelerated aging and disease. "One can thrive on half the normal intake of food as long as we consume high electron-rich nutrients."[4] Any time we put a substance in the body that has a positive charge, we increase the oxidation of the body and therefore accelerate the aging process. As we age, our body's ORP continually rises. The pace at which our body oxidizes is directly related to our diet and the other substances we put in it. Our immediate environment also contributes to the oxidation of the body. Genetics does not determine the rate of oxidation of the body.

Alkaline Ionized Water has a negative ORP, and therefore it offsets the positive ORP of our oxidizing, aging body. Thus, we counteract the aging process by consuming negatively charged substances that dampen the positive ORP of our oxidizing body. Realistically, we need to drink at least one to two gallons of strong Alkaline Ionized Water each day if we expect significant slowing and reversal of the biological aging process, which is determined by the health of our cells. Human health equals cellular health. If our body's cells are healthy, we will be healthy. If they are not healthy, we cannot be healthy.

Consuming fresh Alkaline Ionized Water puts a mild electrical charge into the body the same way raw fruits and vegetables do, which is why we feel energized after eating them. Living foods have this charge because they are full of enzymes, electrons, and electrical activity, which is facilitated by the mineral content of the plants the same way it is for us. Living foods are bio-photonic, meaning they are created by sunlight (photons) and they are alive with enzymatic activity. Living foods are essentially concentrated sunlight. Thus they are bio-electrical, alive with electrical activity. We are also bio-electrical, meaning that electricity conducts through the body when there are sufficient amounts and varieties of minerals present for electricity to flow. If these minerals are absent from the body, it will not function properly. In the total absence of these minerals, the body and its organs will cease to function, and we will die. Minerals are critical to all life.

Strong, fresh Alkaline Ionized Water charges the body because it contains large amounts of electrons that encourage electrical activity in the body. "The more alive something is, the more it is moving from the dense matter of nucleons and protons to the world of light and electrons."[5] The foods and water we consume should contain substances that promote electrical activity within us. They provide us with energy and charge the body's internal battery. Alkaline Ionized Water also has a negative charge, or Oxidation Reduction Potential (ORP), that promotes electrical activity in the body. When the body is charged and has sufficient amounts of electrical activity we feel energetic. The brain cannot operate without electrical activity. Every thought we have produces a miniature electrical storm in various areas of the brain, depending on what the thought is. As we stimulate electrical activity in the brain by consuming substances that encourage electrical activity, we are able to think more clearly. It is this constant recharging of the body through living foods and Alkaline Ionized Water that helps keep us young, active, and disease-free.

ORP is the single most important term we need to become familiar with if we want to understand human health. A person's ORP level, although quite difficult to determine reliably, would instantly reveal whether he or she is in a state of health or disease. ORP is another way to measure the body's vibration. Everything in the universe vibrates. When we are healthy, we vibrate within a certain frequency range. If we are sick, we will vibrate at a completely different frequency range, one that reflects our state of unhealthiness or disease.

ORP is a measurement of a substance's ability to either diminish or encourage the oxidation of another substance. When we consume living foods, they diminish the oxidation of our bodies. Thus, living foods rejuvenate us. Living foods are also negatively charged. Cooking living foods oxidizes them, thus raising their ORP. When we consume cooked foods, we add to the oxidation of our bodies and accelerate the aging process. It encourages disease by acidifying the body. Cooked foods burn us up internally by stimulating oxidation since they themselves have already been oxidized with a positive ORP of +400 mV or higher. Animal protein, fried foods, soft drinks, and other highly processed foods possess the highest ORP and therefore the greatest amount of hydrogen (positive) ions. A high ORP is an *environment* where disease thrives because it is also a high-acid (low pH) *environment.* To reduce this oxidation, this slow-burning fire within us, we must consume substances that possess a negative charge, such as Alkaline Ionized Water and raw fruits and vegetables. When we do, the consuming fire of high ORP is extinguished, and an alkaline environment is created in the body.

The principles of ORP are the same for Alkaline Ionized Water. The positive ORP of *Acid Ionized Water* increases oxidation because it contains hydrogen ions (missing electrons), which is the *environment* of all disease. The negative charge of Alkaline Ionized Water reduces oxidation because it contains hydroxyl ions (extra electrons), which is an *environment* that leads to health.

Consuming Alkaline Ionized Water bathes the interior of the body in a negatively charged liquid, which promotes rejuvenation of each bodily system at a cellular level. For instance, a liver cell is better able to repair itself in a negative ion alkaline environment than a positive ion acid environment. When we consume negatively charged substances such as Alkaline Ionized Water, this oxidation is retarded and our body's cells are in a better position to repair and rejuvenate themselves. Nothing is better for the body.

A fresh glass of strong Alkaline Ionized Water right out of the tap will contain a cloud of tiny bubbles in the water. These are hydroxyl ions, Alkaline Ionized Water's other antioxidant component. The best way to drink Alkaline Ionized Water is as fresh as possible. Drinking cloudy Alkaline Ionized Water with its abundance of electrons is one of the healthiest things we can do.

Some antioxidants possess an extra electron. Others, such as carotenoids, which are natural pigments from foods, retard and reverse aging through chemical processes. Alkaline Ionized Water is an extremely effective antioxidant because it is a liquid with small water molecule clusters, and it is more easily absorbed into the body, where it can be of immediate use.

Antioxidants have anti-aging and anti-disease properties because they help return the body's cells to a youthful, healthier, more natural state. As we make Alkaline Ionized Water a part of our daily routine and drink sufficient quantities of it, we begin to bathe the body's cells in alkalinity and antioxidants, as well as hydrating them better than they have ever been. Nothing could be more fundamentally healthier for us.

Free radicals are another example of an environment that encourages disease in our bodies by causing cellular mutations and other types of cellular damage. Free radical cellular damage is a big part of the aging equation, but it can also be reversed with proper diet and the consistent use of Alkaline Ionized Water.

Free radicals are commonly created from *prescription and street drugs; chemicals (pesticides, herbicides, insecticides, etc.); processed and irradiated foods; food additives and preservatives; heavy metal poisoning; artificial food colorings; polyunsaturated oil, mainly vegetable oils, and rancid oils; trans-fats (partially hydrogenated fats); chlorinated unfiltered tap water; tobacco use; excessive, prolonged stress; cooked foods of all kinds, especially fried foods.*

Alkaline Ionized Water contains high amounts of hydrogen which is one of the keys to its powerful antioxidant capability. Hydrogen is stored in tissue of our body which acts as an antioxidant to protect cells from oxidation. As we age, this store of hydrogen is depleted in the body and must be replaced to stop this oxidation. This can only be accomplished through the daily consumption of Alkaline Ionized Water and raw fruits and vegetables.

Hydrogen converts toxic hydroxyl radicals in the body into stable hydrogen gas, which is found through nature in raw fruits and vegetables. Hydrogen pH stands for "potential hydrogen" or the "potential for freeing hydrogen". In regard to human health, pH should be understood as the number of hydrogen ions in your body. pH is best measured daily through the urine, and not the blood since urine pH reflects your body's overall pH while blood pH always remains stable between 7.25 to 7.45 as a mechanism to bring balance, or homeostasis, to the body.

Highly alkaline foods offer a greater potential for the body to absorb the hydrogen they contain. Hydrogen allows the cells of the body to remain hydrated, toxins to be eliminated and nutrients to be transported to the cells for assimilation. Hydrogen also ensures our joints are lubricated. It allows the body's immune system to form defensive cells that fight bacterial, viral, and fungal infections throughout the body. Hydrogen plays an important role in the production of adenosine triphosphate (ATP), which is where the body gets its energy. Hydrogen ions are transported to the mitochondria of the cells, which then uses the hydrogen to create ATP. Lack of ATP production in the body is why many people constantly feel tired. Ribose, a pentose monosaccharide (simple sugar), is also critical to the production of ATP.

Essentially all disease appears and develops in the body from our diet. Science can determine which genes have been damaged or otherwise altered in an individual, but it has only vague theories as to why and how the defect actually occurred. Environmental diseases may come from sources such as artificial chemical toxins, heavy metals, radiation, naturally occurring toxic substances, or insect-borne diseases, but these can all be battled and often overcome by the right diet, Alkaline Ionized Water, probiotics, exercise, and use of a far infrared (FIR) sauna.

The scientific and medical communities are desperately trying to find a genetic link to every disease, including cancer. It is an effort to establish that disease is born in genetic anomalies and flaws, and thus curing these diseases lies in the engineering and reconstruction of these flawed genes. These efforts manifest themselves in medications and artificial therapies of every kind. All these efforts are enabling devices designed to allow us to keep eating foods that we love and are accustomed to, but unfortunately lead to nearly all disease. The path to health does not lie in these artificial protocols and procedures, nor will it ever. True health is found only in nature where the reflection of God is also found because it is His creation.

Drinking Alkaline Ionized Water gives you energy. On the surface, it seems like an impossible claim that drinking water could possibly give you energy. Once the hydroxyl ions in Alkaline Ionized Water are donated to free radicals, what remains are stable oxygen molecules, which provide the body with more dissolved oxygen. If your blood oxygen level is low, check it before you first start drinking Alkaline Ionized Water and then again a few weeks after you have been drinking it regularly and see the difference for yourself.

Alkalizes and Balances Body pH

The world's written history was recorded on alkaline paper until 1850, when it began to be recorded on paper that used bleach, alum, and tannin in the book-binding, all of which are acid. Those original written documents from 1850 forward are disintegrating at an alarming rate. The best that can be done is to scan them electronically and save what is left of the books by re-alkalizing the remaining paper. However, books printed on alkaline paper before 1850 still survive, often in perfect condition. Acid destroys; a balanced, slightly alkaline pH preserves. Acid destroys life; alkalinity restores and sustains it.

We look everywhere for health when it is never any further than what we put in our body. Alkaline substances belong in the body, not acid ones. *All disease thrives in an acid environment and will not thrive in an, environment.*

If we create an acidic environment in our bodies by years of consuming cooked foods and other acidic substances such as drugs, alcohol, cigarettes, soft drinks, processed sugar, etc., then we become vulnerable to any disease that invades the body, regardless of its source. The more acidic a person is, the more susceptible he or she is to disease. This acid environment does not cause disease but rather creates an environment that disease thrives in. As disease flourishes in the body, it creates a more acidic environment in order to spread further until it consumes the body. Disease is essentially another mechanism nature uses to recycle something that is no longer a part of itself. Yeast, fungus, and mold found in the body are also recycling agents used by nature to dispose of that which no longer belongs to itself. Even if we do have genetic propensities toward certain diseases, those diseases can be prevented and overcome by proper diet and hydration of the body. Other than extremely rare examples, the only instances we find of animals in the wild with chronic disease are those that have been overexposed to synthetic toxins in polluted areas.

One of the keys to great health and honoring our temple is to keep the body pH properly balanced and alkaline. Drinking plenty of Alkaline Ionized Water will help achieve that.

Nearly everything the average person consumes, including cooked and processed foods, acidifies the body tremendously. Nearly all recreational beverages are acidic, including coffee, black tea, commercial juices, sports and energy drinks, milk, soft drinks, and alcohol. Stress adds tremendous amounts of acidity to the body, as does pollution. Industrialization has toxified and acidified our environment since its inception. Given the amount of acidity that is added to the average person on a daily basis, it would be extremely difficult for anyone to over-alkalize their body.

I have consumed 1.5 to 2.0 gallons of Alkaline Ionized Water every day for twelve years at a pH 9.5 or higher. I live on a 99 percent living-food diet, which is alkalizing, and my body pH is always balanced at close to 7.0. I have never measured my body pH and found it to be too alkaline. (See *Appendix Four: Testing Body pH*.) Over-alkalizing your body will not occur if your approach to health is completely natural. Nature always puts the body into balance when its laws are followed, and at the core of homeostasis is a neutral pH. If we wish to determine a person's overall health, the first measurement that should be taken is his or her body pH.

Powerful Detoxifier and Superior Hydrator

Alkaline Ionized Water is sometimes called *cluster water, microwater,* or *microcluster Water* because of its small molecular grouping. Water molecules typically group in clusters of ten and can even chain hundreds of molecules together. *Ionized Water* molecule clusters are grouped into six water molecules, and thus they are *reduced* in size from conventional water molecule clusters. Alkaline Ionized Water molecule cluster has changed from an irregular, clumpy shape to a hexagonal shape that penetrates and saturates body tissue much more efficiently than conventional water.

Water ionizers have more than one level of ionization strength, which is important to some people when they first start drinking it. The strong detoxification aspects of Alkaline Ionized Water require that people with accumulated toxins in their bodies and tissues begin drinking it at a mild ionization level (pH 8.0), then slowly increase the strength of the Alkaline Ionized Water over the following days and weeks until they acclimate to it. When first using Alkaline Ionized Water, *headaches, rashes, diarrhea, and fatigue are common detoxification symptoms* for people who have accumulated toxins throughout their body from poor lifestyle choices such as diet and social habits. These different levels of ionization strength allow people to slowly ease into Alkaline Ionized Water when they first start drinking it in order to mollify these powerful detoxification effects that can be drastic for those who are quite toxic. The micro-cluster structure and penetrating aspects of Alkaline Ionized Water leave less room for anything that does not belong in bodily tissue. Thus toxins are effectively pushed out of the tissue and into the bloodstream to then be eliminated by the body.

The sight of a glass of Alkaline Ionized Water with small bubbles in it is appears innocuous in regard to detoxification. In fact, it is a powerhouse when it comes to getting rid of what is not wanted in the body. A toxin is simply something that does not belong in the body. There are mild toxins and quite dangerous toxins such as heavy metals, asbestos, or industrial chemical residue. The average person can begin drinking Alkaline Ionized Water without having a serious *healing crisis*, which is a term sometimes applied to a strong and immediate detoxification that is usually an unpleasant, if not painful, experience. Those most at risk are people who have taken a lot of street drugs or prescription medications or those whose diets consist primarily of processed, fried, junk, or fast foods. Also at risk of a strong detoxification are those who have been exposed to environmental toxins such as heavy metals, herbicides, and/or pesticides, which are more common than many of us realize.

Alkaline Ionized Water is deceptively powerful because water is not conventionally thought of as a powerful detoxifier. The body removes toxins that have accumulated in it through the lungs, the kidneys, the bowels, and the skin. Alkaline Ionized Water mainly removes toxins from the body through the kidneys and bowels, but also through the skin, which is why drinking it can occasionally give you a short-term rash. All detoxification symptoms, pleasant or unpleasant, are necessary evils that we must go through. Removing poisons from your body after a long time of them being housed there can be a very difficult experience, but in the long run a very healthy one.

As long as we don't consume too much in a short period of time or around mealtime, we cannot drink too much Alkaline Ionized Water once our body has acclimated to it. The more toxins a person has accumulated in his or her flesh, tissue, and cells, the weaker the

Alkaline Ionized Water should be when he or she first starts drinking it so any unpleasant detoxification effects are kept to a minimum. If the detoxification symptoms become too strong, reduce the strength of the Alkaline Ionized Water and drink less of it. If a person maintains a relatively good diet, drinks a lot of water, and doesn't smoke, drink alcohol heavily, take drugs, or medication, he or she can usually start Alkaline Ionized Water at the highest level (pH 9.5–9.9).

Regarding children, the vast majority of them have no trouble drinking Alkaline Ionized Water on the strongest level when they first start because they are too young to have accumulated many toxins in their flesh. Their young, resilient bodies are also able to quickly adjust to the healthy environment that Alkaline Ionized Water creates.

The opposite is true regarding the elderly, who have a lifetime of toxins and heavy metals accumulated in their bodies and are often on medications that also need to be detoxified from their tissue. Children on strong medications or a junk food diet may also suffer these powerful detoxification effects.

A balanced state of health is that in which the body thrives and is most apt to operate to its capacity. However, if you change the body's environment through poor diet, meaning foods that have been oxidized by processing or cooking, a buildup of hydrogen ions results. The consequence of this is an acidic state and a low pH. To be healthy again, you need only change the environment of your body by adding alkaline substances that have an abundance of electrons such as Alkaline Ionized Water and raw fruits and vegetables.

Alkaline Ionized Water reflects the characteristics of living foods in several ways:

- Alkaline Ionized Water has an abundance of electrons, as do living foods.

- Ionized Water has a negative charge, or ORP, as do living foods.
- Alkaline Ionized Water possesses negative ions, as do living foods.
- Alkaline Ionized Water is alkaline, as are living foods.
- Alkaline Ionized Water is hydrating, as are living foods.
- Alkaline Ionized Water is detoxifying, as are living foods.
- Alkaline Ionized Water provides the body with ionic (organic) minerals, as do living foods.

Cooked foods have a deficit of electrons, a positive ORP, and an abundance of positive ions. They are dry and dehydrating. They also acidify and add toxins to the body. All these qualities lead to disease and therefore are the exact opposite of what we should put in the body.

Alkaline Ionized Water mimics many of the same attributes in nature that bring us health. Only nature can bring us true health. Vitamin supplements attempt to mimic nature, although with dismal results. Medicine attempts to overcome the natural mechanisms of the body, in an attempt to control, alter, or outsmart it. Pharmaceuticals only mask symptoms of disease. They endeavor to manage the crisis that is brought about by disease infiltrating and attacking the body. Symptoms are messengers to us that are the result of the disease. If we interpret them correctly, we will begin to understand what we must do to rid the body of that disease. We take drugs that attempt only to send these messengers away. We should embrace them, not cover them up, for they are trying to speak to us. No drug has yet been invented that cures the body of any disease, nor will one ever be. Pharmaceuticals never lead to health but only allow people to hobble along a little further as they become sicker until the quality of their lives diminish to a point where the option of death is more appealing than continuing to live with such agony. Disease is a symptom that an imbalance in the body exists. True health is only found in nature because it is God's creation. Alkaline Ionized Water mimics and magnifies the qualities of nature better than any substance known.

How Long Ionized Water **Lasts**

Alkaline Ionized Water

- Hydroxyl ions: ten to twenty minutes
- *(A small number will remain up to twenty-four hours)*
- Negative ORP (mV charge): eighteen to twenty-four hours
- Alkalinity (high pH): three to eight days
- Smaller molecule clusters: four to eighteen months

Acid Ionized Water

Up to 150 days if stored in a cool, dark place, unopened. Exposing acid Ionized Water to the air:

- Hydrogen ions: thirty to ninety minutes
- *(A small number will remain up to twenty-four hours)*
- High Positive ORP (mV charge): forty-eight to ninety-six hours
- Acidity (low pH): seven to fourteen days
- Smaller molecule clusters: eight to twenty-four months

Why Christians Should Fast

After fasting forty days and forty nights, he was hungry. (Matthew 4:2 NIV)

Fasting is mentioned thirty-eight times in the Bible in nineteen different books.[6] Fasting is absolutely the *best* thing you can do for your health at any given time. When you stop eating, you return your body to the healing hands of God, if only for a short period of time. If you are sick, fasting is the quickest way back to health, a shortcut that allows the body to focus on one thing: not digesting food or taking in nutrients, but that of healing itself. Digestion requires a lot of energy from the body. "Fasting is the great remedy. The physician within!"[7] The best fast you can do is a water fast, and the best water for fasting is Alkaline Ionized Water.

Fasting gives the body a chance to rest, cleanse, and repair itself. Every major religion in the world promotes fasting. Jesus, Buddha, Krishna, prophets, and many other spiritual figures through the ages fasted regularly. Fasting is mentioned in the Bible numerous times in both the Old and New Testaments.

You can fast for any length of time over six hours, which would be considered a mini-fast. Fasting one day a month is a great habit to develop. I fast for twenty-four hours quite often by eating a meal in the evening and then not eating again until the same time the following day. The habit of eating one large meal a day, usually in the late afternoon or early evening, was commonly practiced by ancient warriors, including the Romans, especially before a battle. Fighting on an empty stomach was easier, in part because the body is not burdened with the energy demands of digestion.

The word *breakfast* means to *break a fast*. Instead of eating something for breakfast, I continue my fast for as long as possible by drinking only water in the morning and often into the early hours of the afternoon. Therefore, I fast for at least fourteen hours each day.

Fasting cleanses the body as well as the brain. Clear-minded thinking occurs when the stomach is clear; clouded thinking occurs when the stomach is full.

There are many types of fasting and many ways to fast. For instance, one can fast with *spirulina* and *chlorella*, which is extremely cleansing and energizing. I fasted on *spirulina* and *chlorella* for ten days and never had so much energy in my life. A raw juice fast will produce similar results but is not as intense or cleansing. There are green-vegetable fasts and citrus-juice fasts, but these are not true fasts because we are still putting food into the body. The only *true fast* is a *water fast*.

What you fast on will determine how quickly you expel toxins from your body. For instance, a juice fast will remove two to twenty days of accumulated toxins in a day, whereas an Alkaline Ionized Water fast will remove up to one hundred days of accumulated toxins in a single day.

If you experience severe headaches, rashes, cramps, stomach or joint pain, dizziness, body aches, or nausea, then you are detoxifying too quickly and you need to slow down. The rewards of fasting are many, but it can be a rigorous and painful experience for those who are quite toxic. If you don't feel good while fasting or the pain becomes too intense, then eat something mild such as soup or potatoes and the pain will subside. You will know best when it is time to pull back on the reins.

Detoxification stops immediately when we eat cooked foods of any kind. Cooked foods contain toxins that further poison the body. By eating cooked foods the body has no choice but to stop ridding itself of substances that do not belong in it because more are being added to it.

If you don't feel that you can go it alone, there are clinics and fasting retreat centers that will help you get through a fast. Some people recommend that fasts be supervised in order to make it easier for the person fasting to go through it because of the reassurance and support it can offer. Pain is easier when the sufferer has a hand to hold and shoulder to brace him or herself on.

If you decide to fast, try to get some support from those around you. Ask them not to encourage you to eat something even though you may be hungry. After fasting for a couple days, your hunger will disappear, although you will still miss the habit of simply putting something in your mouth. Without a doubt, fasting is the best way to jumpstart your health. The advice I have for anyone who is sick, regardless of the disease, is to fast. Fasting cleanses our temple faster than anything else we can do for it.

Acid Ionized Water
(External Use Only)

When Acid Ionized Water is freshly produced, the small bubbles found in the water are free radicals, which is why Acid Ionized Water should never be consumed. Acid Ionized Water is also an oxidant because it has a high positive charge or ORP (+700 to 800 mV), which is detrimental to our health. We must avoid substances that encourage oxidation, such as cooked foods and Acid Ionized Water. As with Acid Ionized Water, the water temperature and flow rate through the water ionizer are components that will also determine its strength.

We have a symbiotic relationship with trees and plants of every kind. We breathe in the oxygen that they exhale while they breathe in the carbon dioxide that we exhale. A plant's growth and health are significantly enhanced with the regular use of Acid Ionized Water, and these benefits are unmistakable.

I left my prized hang-basket potted herb garden in the July sun too long one day and forgot to water it. When I found it, the soil was bone dry, and every plant was wilted beyond recognition. The desiccated greenish leaves hung over the sides like spaghetti. I could see it was gone. It was in the upper nineties and the basket had been out all day without a drop of water for two days. I took it inside, saturated the leaves, roots, and soil with Acid Ionized Water, and placed it in the shade. I thought it would help, but I thought it was too late to revive it. However, within three hours of watering it with Acid Ionized Water, it was completely rejuvenated, as though nothing had ever happened to it. Something that we thought was on its way to the grave had indeed been resurrected.

If strong enough, Acid Ionized Water can kill bacteria on contact. This would require a pH of 6.0 or lower. How effective it is as a disinfectant depends on the strength of the Acid Ionized Water, meaning how high the ORP (mV) and how low the pH is. Mild Acid Ionized Water produced from tap water using a home water ionizer typically has a range of 700 to 950 mV (pH 4.0–5.8), which is quite effective at killing surface bacteria and retarding its growth. It is the high charge, or ORP, in the water that is the major factor in killing bacteria followed by an extremely low pH environment.

Acid Ionized Water has a wonderful conditioning effect on the skin and hair because they both are somewhat acidic. Acidic skin is the body's first line of defense against bacteria. Human skin typically has a pH of 5.4 in order to ward off bacteria and infection, and hair typically has a pH of 5.6, although these can vary slightly between individuals.

Applying Acid Ionized Water regularly to the skin works as an astringent to tighten it and help remove wrinkles, leaving no chemical residue as other astringents do. The only residue on the skin is water, which of course is harmless. Acid Ionized Water soothes and helps keep the skin clear of acne and other blemishes. Skin and hair, even animal fur, respond positively to the conditioning effects of Acid Ionized Water. The more Acid Ionized Water that is applied on the skin and hair, the better they respond to it, and there is no limit to the number of applications one can have each day. Acid Ionized Water does have a slight drying effect on the skin, which is why you may want to apply a moisturizer such as shea butter.

Combined with drinking Acid Ionized Water, which alkalizes the body internally, skin conditions of every kind such as shingles are dramatically improved. However, this can be short-lived if the root of the problem is not addressed by a fundamental change in diet. For instance, a condition such as psoriasis arises from a poor diet of junk foods and excessive animal protein. Chronic skin problems are a result of toxins making their way to the skin on their way out of the body. People with chronic skin conditions go through life using ointments and creams that allay the symptoms of their disease without ever treating its cause. If the diet is not changed to include more alkaline foods, Acid Ionized Water will at best only temporarily relieve skin conditions such as *psoriasis*. In fact, in the case of psoriasis, Acid Ionized Water can appear to worsen the condition.

Rashes, cuts, scrapes, even serious wounds, as well as athlete's foot and other fungus, are dramatically improved with the application of Acid Ionized Water. It takes the itch out of mosquito bites and alleviates the pain of stings and other insect bites. It provides relief from poison oak and poison ivy exposure. It is especially effective if the affected area is allowed to soak in Acid Ionized Water for twenty to thirty minutes. Excessively dry skin is best treated by soaking it in Acid Ionized Water. This is also true of the deep cuts near the fingernail that people experience in extremely cold, dry weather, which will heal in a few days after soaking them in Acid Ionized Water for twenty to thirty minutes. I would also recommend a natural moisturizer such as shea butter.

Scalp problems such as dandruff are improved with the consistent use of Acid Ionized Water. Eating a proper diet comprised of *spirulina, chlorella,* raw fruits and vegetables, as well as drinking Alkaline Ionized Water, can entirely eliminate many of these health problems. Health problems are an indication that key nutrients in the diet are missing and that your temple is not properly hydrated. Restoration of the body, our temple, occurs when the health protocols of this book are followed.

Acid Ionized Water has been used successfully in treating diabetic skin ulcers, wounds that open up on the skin, particularly the extremities, due to poor circulation. Drinking Alkaline Ionized Water is a great benefit to diabetics because it helps bring the body into pH balance and provides it with lots of oxygen, which increases circulation. Once again, changing the environment of the body with negatively charged hydroxyl ions and electrons helps bring it into a position where it can defend and heal itself.

Acid Ionized Water can be applied to an incredible array of practical and effective applications, from skin care and treatment to enhanced plant cultivation. It also has great potential for use in the agriculture industry. Acid Ionized Water is an inexpensive, environmentally neutral technology that will one day become as common as chemical applications are today.

Chapter 3

Our Temple Requires
Powerful Whole Food Nutrients

This will bring health to your body and nourishment
to your bones. (Proverbs 3:8 NIV)

A building constructed from inferior materials is ready to collapse at any
moment, if not from external pressures, then from within. The body
built of inferior materials awaits the same fate. The basic elements of
the human cell must be constructed from the exact nutrients it requires
or it will weaken, malfunction and fold under the attack of any disease.

Spirulina and Chlorella: The Foundation of Nutrition

The nutritional content of *spirulina* or *chlorella* makes them the
most powerful foods God has created. No other foods can possibly
compete with their broad array of dense nutritional force. They are the
heavyweights of nutritious superfoods. All grasses such as wheat, barley,
rye, and kamut are incredible foods, but they don't begin to compare to
the nutritional density and power of algae. The greater array of nutrients
a food has, the healthier it is. Of the nearly seventy thousand species of
algae that exist, most are quite nutritious, a few are toxic, and a few are

powerful nutraceuticals capable of providing the body with an array of nutrients that no other foods can.

Spirulina and *chlorella* are complete whole foods, true superfoods. They have a balanced compliment of protein (60 percent), carbohydrates (19 percent), fats (6 percent), bio-available minerals (8 percent), and moisture (7 percent). The protein, carbohydrates, and fat content in *spirulina* and *chlorella* are in the correct natural ratio to one another. They are *not* extracts, concentrates, or amalgams of nutrients that look good on paper such as what appears in vitamin and mineral supplements that are supposedly healthy. In reality, the body does not absorb 90 percent of those kinds of supplements because they are dead. Their enzymes, which are the life force of the food, have been removed. Eating *spirulina* or *chlorella,* on the other hand, is like eating any other whole food such as an apple, orange, or broccoli.

The species of these two algae that I speak of in this book are *Spirulina platensis* and *Chlorella sorokiniana* (formally *pyrenoidosa*). Another *chlorella* product found on the market is *Chlorella vulgaris,* which is nutritionally quite similar to its cousin *sorokiniana* although it does not have as much of the incredible dietary fiber as *sorokiniana.*

A tremendous amount of scientific research has been done on both *spirulina* and *chlorella* from universities and medical institutions around the world. They are also used globally as livestock feed. Once tableted, they will last up to three years when refrigerated and up to fifteen years if it has been vacuum-packed. Both spirulina and chlorella have proven to be one of the best solutions to world food shortages.

We are a society that has come to expect health from a pill. Pharmaceuticals and the medical establishment that pursues, promotes, and profits from them are more to blame for this than anything else because they have convinced so many people that health and the cure for disease come from a pill. People believe that if a small pill can control their cholesterol or high blood pressure, then similarly it must follow that a pill can provide their bodies with all the vitamins, minerals and other nutrients that they are missing from their poor diet. We take vitamin/mineral supplements expecting to be healthy for the same reason. How pharmaceuticals can be so small yet so profoundly alter our physiology is that they are potent poisons and we can only tolerate extremely small amounts of them. Pharmaceuticals try to overcome the natural mechanisms of the body and outsmart disease through artificial methods. As they treat symptoms in one area of the body, they cause problems in other areas, commonly known as side effects.

Almost all vitamin supplements are derived from dead sources that have no enzymes, which is why most end up in your toilet or lodged in your bodily tissue instead of being absorbed and used by the body's cells. The nutrients from living foods such as *spirulina* and *chlorella* are absorbed by the body because of the presence of enzymes in the food. They can be taken in powder or tablets for convenience. It's easy to grab a handful of tablets and pop them down either with a meal or when I'm feeling a little tired. They are the ultimate fast food that is actually healthy.

Some people expect that a few grams of *spirulina* and *chlorella* each day will turn their health around, straighten out their digestive problems, and give them a lot more energy. However, you should recognize them for what they are—whole foods, not supplements or stimulants and certainly not drugs that react with the body instead of providing it with nutrients. Viewing them this way makes us realize what an incredibly small amount of food they actually are. You would not expect to gain any significant health benefits from that amount of any other foods such as a banana, parsley, steak, or fish, for example. Yet, even that small amount of algae contains a considerable amount of nutritional potential, more than any other whole food. Viewing it from that perspective, you can understand why you will never receive a better nutritional value than by using *spirulina* and/or *chlorella*.

The Power Triad of Nutrition

Spirulina and *chlorella* contain three components in greater concentrations than any other whole foods: protein (amino acids), nucleic acids (RNA/DNA), and chlorophyll. They are also the three most important nutrients required by the body. They build our health in a fundamental way, including structural and cardiovascular foundations of our health. They are also responsible for growth, cleansing, repair, and overall bodily maintenance.

Spirulina and *chlorella* are complete proteins because they provide the body with the nine essential amino acids, yet they go much further. Their complement of eighteen amino acids are in a natural ratio to one another. Animal protein, on the other hand, has a limited complement of amino acids that are heavily weighted in some, yet drastically low in others. This is one reason why the body does not react well to them and why they lead to so many diseases. For instance, taking a large dose of only one amino acid such as L-tryptophan has the potential of causing serious health problems, even death.[8]

There is a lot of confusion and misinformation about protein, how much is in certain foods, and what their amino acid structure actually consists of. It is assumed that meat is comprised mostly of protein when it is only 15 to 20 percent protein on average. Beef, for instance, has eleven amino acids and is heavily weighted in four of them, which is a lopsided amino acid complement. Chicken has fifteen times the amount of methionine, a sulfur-based amino acid, than beef. What the body requires is a broad array of amino acids that are in correct proportions to one another such as that found in *spirulina* and *chlorella*.

Even wheat grass juice is only 20 percent protein compared to over 60 percent for *spirulina* and *chlorella*, the highest percentage of protein of any whole foods. Evenly proportioned amino acid structures are common throughout the plant world. However, no other food contains the incredibly high percentage, variety, and even complement of amino acids than algae. In the world of human nutrition, *spirulina* and *chlorella* are the undisputed heavyweight champions.

As we take a few grams of algae each day, we begin to realize that a remarkably small amount of food provides the body with the greatest nutritional punch of any whole food known. Most importantly, however, is that when the body is getting sufficient amounts of protein in the correct amino acid structure, it now begins to function exactly as it should, that of a state of health.

Animal Protein vs. Plant Protein

In general, cooked-food vegetarians don't get enough protein in their diet, which is a major problem that can lead to fatigue, anemia, and many other health problems. Often people will simply remove meat, fish, eggs, and dairy from their diet and become strict vegetarians or vegans. This is a big mistake because protein is essential to the body in every way since it is the building blocks of our cells. A severe lack of protein in the body will lead to *cachexia,* where the organs are robbed of protein in order to perform bodily functions similar to the way osteoporosis robs the bones of calcium for bodily needs.

A diet comprised of mostly living (raw) foods provides the body with a sufficient, but not ideal, amount of protein. The body cannot store protein and will easily rid itself of any excess protein when it is derived from living foods, not cooked animal-food sources. Excessive animal protein, on the other hand, will lead to severe imbalances in the body, including *ketosis, uremia,* and a host of other diseases. A high-protein diet results in increased acidity in the body and is easily as punishing and destructive to the body as malnourishment is to it.

Sufficient amounts of protein *must* be consumed with every meal in order for the food to properly digest and its nutrients to be efficiently extracted and absorbed by the body. Digestion does not require a large amount of protein. Rather, the key is that you consume high-quality plant protein with a broad array of amino acids that are in the correct ratio to one another. *Spirulina* and *chlorella* fit the bill perfectly. Only 3 to 6 grams of *spirulina* and *chlorella* (1.8–3.6 grams of protein) are needed with each meal to fulfill the protein needs of proper digestion. To exceed that amount would enhance algae's digestive and other nutritional components. Both cooked and living foods are digested better and more nutrients are extracted from them when a sufficient amount of protein is present. This is especially true of plant protein such as that found in algae.

Animal protein that has been denatured by cooking is a great detriment to the body. The antibiotics, hormones, and steroids that are injected into commercial livestock can adversely affect the growth of children and destroy the friendly bacteria that the human body requires for digestion. Animal protein must be broken down into basic amino acids to be re-formed into protein chains that can then be used by the human body. This is a laborious and inefficient process that robs the body of energy and resources rather than nutrifies it. The biggest culprit is meat because it is so difficult to digest.

I give every green plant for food. (Genesis 1:30 NIV)

Meat is the centerpiece of the average diet out of tradition, conditioning (we are all raised on meat), convenience, but mostly taste.

People love the taste of meat, especially when it has a lot of fat. Meat by itself is actually quite flawless. However, the Bible encourages the vegetarian diet. Genesis 1:29 tells us that every fruit and vegetable is provided to us by God.

> Everything that lives and moves will be food for you. Just as I gave you the green plants, I now give you everything. But you must not eat meat that has its lifeblood still in it. (Genesis 9:3–4 NIV)

Meat is quite difficult to digest and can remain in the digestive tract for days, even weeks. Meat contains no dietary fiber, which is one of the reasons it is so difficult to digest. Like all cooked foods, meat is void of enzymes and therefore is not self-digesting. All animal food sources are quite acidic to the body, which is one of their worst characteristics.

The higher you eat on the food chain, the greater the concentration of toxins you put in your body. Meat is at the top of the food chain and therefore is the most toxic food we consume. Fish have high concentrations of heavy metals, such as mercury.[9] This is especially true of swordfish, shark, mackerel, tuna, or any of the other large sea or freshwater fish. Pregnant women in particular should avoid these fish because of the potential of heavy metal poisoning of their fetus. All poisons concentrate at higher levels in smaller creatures, such as a fetus. The smaller a living being is, the more susceptible they are to toxicity.

Since eggs and dairy products come directly from animals, they are next on the list of foods that have high concentrations of toxins. Animals eat thousands of these meals throughout their lives, and these toxins have concentrated throughout their bodies. As cattle graze on land that has been sprayed with herbicides and pesticides, toxins accumulate in their flesh up to twenty-five times the concentration of those found in the grass they graze on. Therefore, when you consume that beef, you are eating a food that are twenty-five times more concentrated than the grass they lived on. Liver is the worst animal food that can be consumed because it has the highest concentration of toxins in it since it is the toxin filter for the body. Long considered a power food because of the high amount of iron it contains, liver should be considered a food of *last* resort.

Dairy products lead to allergies and mucus buildup in the body, in part because of the extremely high amount of casein found in milk, up to twenty times that found in human milk. Casein is a polymer that acts as a binder to form mucus. Mucus first fills the lungs and then the sinuses, which can lead to sinus headaches and infections, as well as intensifying allergies. Sinus infections and sinus headaches are caused from the sinus cavities being impacted with mucous.

We are the only species that consumes milk from another species, and we are the only species that consumes milk past infancy. No one would consider drinking a tall glass of human milk but think nothing of consuming milk from an animal that smells so bad most people don't want to be anywhere near them. Human milk is full of nutrients and hormones and is meant to be consumed by a human infant.

The protein content of mother's milk varies greatly from species to species and speaks volumes about why milk should only be consumed by the species it is meant for. Human milk is less than 1 percent protein, while cow's milk is over 15 percent, which accounts for one reason why they grow to adulthood much quicker than humans.

Milk has the great advantage of being white, and like most things that are white, it is therefore deemed to be good, and therefore healthy. We are conditioned to believe that dairy products are healthy and provide us with significant amounts of calcium, which is a huge myth.[10] If this were the case, then the people of nations where dairy products are not consumed would have low bone density, but just the opposite is true. Denmark, Norway, and Holland consume the *most* dairy products in the world and have the *highest* cases of osteoporosis, bone disease, heart disease, and breast cancer.[11] Countries such as Gambia, where no dairy products are consumed, have the highest bone density in the world.[12]

When a baby is born, mother's milk provides the perfect complement of protein, carbohydrates, fat, minerals, digestive enzymes, vitamins, hormones, immunoglobulins, and antibodies. The central purpose of milk is that of a hormonal/nutrient delivery system. When we drink the milk from another animal such as a cow, we are delivering to the human body many things that only belong in that animal, including hormones, which are instructional messengers. When you consume animal milk, your body is receiving hormonal instructions from another species. Cow's milk has fifty-nine hormones while human milk has only twenty-three hormones. This highlights how out of place another species' milk is in our human bodies.

Dairy products are unhealthy substances that we have been conditioned to believe are healthy. Few of us ever stop to consider why we would want to put what is meant for the infant of another animal into our human body. Dairy products are at the top of our list of foods to remove from our diet as we begin our new life of true health.

Miracle of the Temple: Curing Disease

It is one hundred times easier to prevent a disease than it is to cure the body of one. However, once the body has acquired a disease, much larger doses of powerful whole foods such as *spirulina* and *chlorella* will be required to rid the body of disease. This highlights the importance of making *spirulina* and *chlorella* a regular part of the diet before the onset of disease.

A major cause of disease can be traced back to excessive free radicals in the body and a lack of antioxidants to neutralize them. Premature aging also comes from a lack of nucleic acids and other nutrients that are capable of rebuilding the cell that can only be derived from living foods.

A *growth factor* in health and nutrition refers to a substance that builds the immune system. *Chlorella* has the ability to quadruple in quantity every twenty hours, which no other plant on earth can do. It is programmed into its DNA, and it is the *chlorella growth factor* (CGF) that is responsible for this ability. CGF causes children and young animals to grow at an accelerated rate and damaged tissue to significantly increase its rate of healing.

Children fed *chlorella* in a long-term study had healthy, cavity-free teeth, fewer colds, and improved intellectual capacity. The children, who were chosen because they were smaller than they should have been for their age, more than made up for their disadvantages and even grew taller than other children in the control group who were not fed CGF.[13]

CGF stimulates tissue repair, even if it has been ulcerated or damaged and has resisted traditional healing methods. It can even be used topically on cuts and lacerations to accelerate healing. CGF has proven effective against memory loss, depression, and other psychiatric diseases.

CGF improves our immune system and strengthens our body's ability to recover from exercise and disease. It helps prevent gastric ulcers and promotes healthy pregnancies. In experiments, mice that were injected with cancer cells showed a high resistance to the cancer when they were fed *chlorella*. It is the CGF in *chlorella* that stimulates B-cell, macrophage, and interferon production, which has natural anti-cancer properties. Consuming 3 to 6 grams of CGF powder daily also results in high energy levels throughout the day.

CGF is unique to *chlorella* and present in the greatest values in the strain *Pyrenoidosa*. CGF still holds many secrets, but what is known is that it contains a nucleotide-peptide complex that performs small miracles in the body. RNA/DNA (nucleic acids) are responsible for directing cellular renewal, growth, and repair. They are the blueprints to our cells and were identified as essential nutrients in 1990. CGF is the only plant extract I recommend.

RNA/DNA also strengthens immunity by invigorating T-cells and B-cells that are the principal immune system defenders against viruses and other invading microorganisms. CGF is responsible for the production of macrophages within the immune system that can assist in the destruction of cancer cells and the removal of cellular debris throughout the body. CGF promotes normal growth but does not stimulate the growth of disease processes such as tumors.

High-Energy Superfoods

One of the biggest complaints from people who subsist on a typical cooked-food diet is that they are constantly tired and sapped of energy. *Spirulina* is the highest energy food I know of. It is packed with the vitamin B complex, which is synonymous with high energy. The ample protein content of *spirulina* and *chlorella* also provides the body with lots of natural energy. If we rebuild the cells with sufficient amounts of nucleic acids and protein, the body will feel more energetic.

I take 5 grams of *spirulina* sixty minutes every before workout, and the difference is unmistakable. I can exercise harder, for a longer period of time, and recover quicker when I take *spirulina* before a workout. Athletes who have discovered these superfoods and pre-load on them before training or competition have a decided edge over those who don't.

Spirulina and *chlorella* have the broadest array of nutrients of any foods known. I am a firm believer that we need to get as many different types of foods into our diet as possible. Eating a banana, broccoli, and a radish in a single day is great, but eating ten or twenty other types of living foods in the same day would be even better. It is not the volume of food but rather the diversity of plant foods and whether they are raw, not cooked or processed, that is important.

One can live indefinitely on either *spirulina* or *chlorella* and be quite healthy because they are such nutritionally diverse foods. *Spirulina* contains gamma-linolenic acid (GLA), an essential fatty acid that is excellent for the treatment of arthritis. *Spirulina* is 95 percent digestible, higher than any food known. It contains more beta-carotene than any other whole food, as well as ninety-two trace minerals and other nutritional elements such as vitamins, chlorophyll, *glycolipids*, *phycocyanin, carotenoids,* and *sulfolipids.* It is also abundant in the antioxidant *superoxide dismutase* (SOD)

Spirulina and *chlorella* are superfoods that are known as *nutraceuticals.* A nutraceutical is any food that provides the body with the proper nutrients that the body can use to heal itself and prevent disease. No food, including *spirulina* and *chlorella,* will ever heal the body, nor will any food that we consume for that matter. Rather, it is the nutrients that the body absorbs from living foods that it will use to heal itself from internal or external damage. A true nutraceutical can only come from a living whole food, one that has not been processed, heated, or irradiated in any way that would damage or destroy its enzymes and organic chemical substances, all of which are quite delicate.

Spirulina and *chlorella* are nutritionally dense foods with an incredibly broad array of nutrients that genuinely qualifies them as *superfoods.* Some foods are nutritionally dense, but they do not have a broad array of nutrients.

One could live exclusively on *spirulina* and *chlorella* and be quite healthy, as I did for ten days. I was cleansing with water and fiber from algae as well as rebuilding my body with its nutrients. It brought me to another level of health I had not experienced before. I learned that it is not as much the quantity of any living food we put into our body to build it but the quality. Quantity has almost nothing to do with it when it comes to health. The cooked-food world is one of dieting, label reading, and calorie counting. That is why *spirulina* and *chlorella* are such perfect foods to fast with. They are low calorie, nutrient-dense living foods that demonstrate without any doubt that nutrition is not about volume but rather about density and variety of nutrients in any given food that makes them healthy.

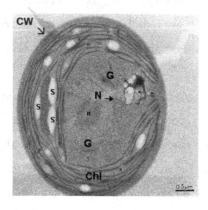

Chlorella is *the* most powerful healing food known. It has tremendous anti-cancer properties. It also has tremendous liver-cleansing and healing abilities. *Chlorella* can be used topically on cuts, rashes, and even serious wounds to increase healing. Wounds react wonderfully when they have direct access to the nucleic acids RNA/DNA in *chlorella*. *Spirulina* can also be used externally on abrasions and serious wounds. Whether taken internally or used externally, algae provides the body and its myriad cells with the nutrients it needs so it can heal itself.

When you detoxify, you are cleaning the garbage out of your temple. Headaches, body aches, rashes, fatigue, and diarrhea are the classic symptoms of detoxification. They can become severe because the accumulated toxins are dug into the body's tissue. They are bound and in some cases are deeply embedded in the tissue. They house themselves inside the cells themselves and are not easily removed.

The stronger the food, the stronger the detoxification properties it has. Each and every *raw food* has its own detoxification qualities; however, *spirulina* and *chlorella* have the strongest and broadest matrix of detoxification potential. They are capable of removing more toxins from the body than any other whole foods. Cooked foods have the opposite effect because they deposit toxins in the body rather than remove them, which is another reason why they are not rejuvenating in any way.

The fiber in *chlorella* is famous for removing heavy metals and other synthetic toxins from the body. The characteristics of this fiber are unique to *chlorella* and why it so important that we consistently have *chlorella* in our diet because it is not found in any other food source.

The Japanese were the first to discover the incredible detoxifying properties of *chlorella* to remove poisonous substances such as radiation from the body. After atomic weapons were dropped on Hiroshima and Nagasaki, *chlorella* was used to remove radiation from the bodies of those who had become contaminated. *Chlorella* soaks up radiation like a sponge. Alkaline Ionized Water is also useful for the removal of radiation from the body, as is a *far-infrared (FIR) sauna.* Far infrared rays penetrate deeply into bodily tissue to release toxins accumulated in the cells. *Chlorella's* cell-wall fiber binds with toxic substances such as mercury and effectively removes them from the body through the bowels.

Chlorella also readily removes lead, uranium,[14] dioxins, and cadmium from the body. *Spirulina* also has strong detoxification properties, but of a different kind. It has been shown to be extremely effective in removing arsenic from the body. *Spirulina* is a terrific blood purifier and blood builder. *Spirulina* expels many other types of toxins from the body in various ways, which is an advantage in consuming foods that contain a broad and diverse array of nutrients.

Both *spirulina* and *chlorella* have extraordinary healing properties. Consistent use of them will prevent a host of health ailments by ridding the body of toxic substances that are potentially dangerous to it.

Chlorella is one of the best digestive foods known. The incredibly detoxifying fiber in *chlorella* is also a unique dietary fiber unlike that found in any other food. Dietary fiber is critical to human health. Without sufficient levels of fiber in the diet, great health is not possible.

The chlorophyll in *chlorella* helps keep the bowels clean. *Chlorella* has four components that work in harmony to cleanse and detoxify the colon: protein, CGF, fiber, and chlorophyll. Chlorophyll is one of the most detoxifying substances known, cleansing the liver and bloodstream in addition to feeding our intestinal flora.

Chlorella helps restore bowel regularity, normalizes beneficial bowel flora, and promotes detoxification of the bowel.[15] The simple fact that *spirulina* and *chlorella* are unprocessed *foods* enhances their digestibility tremendously, as do all living foods, but none better than algae.

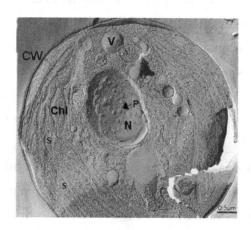

Chlorophyll is perhaps the most important nutrient for the body. *Chlorella* gets its name from the huge amount of chlorophyll in it, the highest of any food known. Chlorophyll's role in human health cannot be understated. It performs many functions throughout the body, including being a heavyweight detoxifier and powerful blood cleanser. For this reason, chlorophyll is often referred as the "blood of plants."

Vegetarians often do not get enough vitamin B12, which is found in meat, fish, eggs, dairy, some sea vegetables, nutritional yeast, algae and fermented soy foods. A vitamin B12 deficiency can lead to anemia and eventually blindness. Symptoms are fatigue, nausea, depression, poor memory and constipation. *Spirulina* and *chlorella* are extremely high in the entire vitamin B complex. One study that used only vegan living foodists concluded that *chlorella* was an excellent source of vitamin B12.[16] Another study done in Japan confirmed the same findings.[17] *Spirulina* has also been proven to be an excellent source of vitamin B12.[18] B vitamins are much more effective if they are all consumed together. For example, vitamin B12 shots are often given to those suffering from anemia. Although it may be of some limited help in the short term, one shot of vitamin B12 is not nearly as effective as eating a raw whole food that contains the entire vitamin B complex such as algae do.

Fat is critical to our health. When a fat molecule comes in contact with a human cell, profound changes occur. Whether that fat molecule is a nutrient or not will determine whether its effect on the body is positive or negative. Essential fatty acids (EFAs)[19] perform a huge number of crucial functions in the body. Without sufficient amounts of fat in our diet, we would become sick and die in a short period of time. Fatty acids are the building blocks of fats in the same way amino acids are the building blocks of proteins. Animal fat is significantly inferior to fat found in most raw plants and does little for our health because it is mostly saturated fat. Foods such as *spirulina* and *chlorella* contain vastly superior types of essential fatty acids.

Gamma linolenic acid (GLA) is found in great abundance in *spirulina* and is beneficial in treating arthritis and rheumatoid disease. *Spirulina* is also high in the omega 6, omega 3, and monoenoic family of EFAs.

Spirulina and *chlorella* did not earn the title of *superfoods* because they might be beneficial to one person but not another. They earned that title because they are the most perfect foods known, containing ideal complements of amino acids (predigested proteins), carbohydrates, and fats. A person could not only survive by exclusively eating these superfoods; he or she would be incredibly healthy in doing so. Ideally, however, we should consume a broad array of living foods in order to obtain optimal health, not limit ourselves to certain food groups.

Spirulina and *chlorella* are not supplements. Supplements are collections of vitamins, minerals, proteins, and other dead nutrients. While their profile may look good on the back nutritional panel of their container, in reality these nutrients will not be assimilated by the body the way nutrients from living foods will. We are not what we eat but what we assimilate. There is no substitute for what God provides for us by way of living food nutrients, nor is the variety limited in any way. The cooked and processed foods that we know and regularly consume are but a slight fraction of the plethora of foods that are available worldwide. The average person has a pathetically limited variety of foods in their diet, typically no more than twenty.

Supplements are produced from extracts and concentrates, which are not alive and have no place in the world of great health. *Spirulina* and *chlorella* are often referred to as supplements, even by prominent naturalists, but this is a misnomer. For instance, I eat three to five cloves of garlic each day. One could say I am supplementing my diet with garlic, but that does not mean that raw garlic itself should be referred to as a supplement because I am eating a whole food. If you were to extract the oil or specific nutrients from garlic and consume it, then that would be considered a supplement. But when the food is consumed whole with nothing extracted from it, it is *not* a supplement.

When algae is harvested fresh, and then either powdered or tableted, it is essentially unchanged from its original state and therefore must still be categorized as a food, not a supplement. Be sure the *spirulina* and *chlorella* that you consume does not use heat in its processing. *Spirulina* and *chlorella* are whole foods, and eating them is like eating a banana, broccoli, or an apple. You can use them to complement your diet with the protein and other broad array of nutrients they possess, but they should always be called what they truly are: *God's most powerful whole foods.*

Chapter 4

Our Temple Requires Living Foods

Then God said, "I give you every seed-bearing plant on the face of the whole earth and every tree that has fruit with seed in it. They will be yours for food. (Genesis 1:29 NIV)

Life cannot come from dead things. Only life begets life. And when a living, raw food is cooked, it is transformed from a rejuvenating nutraceutical to mere sustenance. Cooked foods are dead because they have been raised above a temperature of 118°F. Heat is something that we must have to survive, but when we heat our food, we destroy its enzymes and therefore its life-giving properties. The only foods we should consume are unadulterated living foods that God grows for us and are not compromised by cooking or processing. After all, God grows fruits and vegetables while we are the ones who invented the frying pan. A cooked or processed food provides the body with calories that allows it to keep living tomorrow and next week, but it does not renew the body, our temple, or its cells. Cooked foods also acidify and deposit their toxins in the body, creating the perfect environment for disease to thrive in.

Nowhere in the Bible does it instruct us not to eat cooked foods. Jesus Himself ate fish and bread on several occasions. What His diet was on the whole we do not know.

Plants transform inorganic chemicals into active, living bio-nutrients that have been energized by the sun. Living foods are sun-fired. They are concentrated sunlight in myriad forms of foods that we consume. Plants absorb sunlight and transform its photons into chlorophyll and many other organic chemicals that we absorb when we consume them raw. Therefore, it can be said that, indirectly, we are creations of rearranged sunlight. When we consume foods that have been cooked and destroyed by heat, we remove that food's original nutritional content so it no longer remotely resembles the power of captured, concentrated sunlight it once had. It is no different than if we were to cover ourselves with a blanket to get a suntan and wonder why our skin remains white. Like the blanket that blocks the sun's rays so it cannot tan the skin, heating our food robs the sun of its power to keep us healthy through living foods.

The main reason we need to consume living foods is because they contain enzymes, which are unique to all living things and cannot be reproduced or synthesized. Enzymes catalyze, or speed up, chemical reactions within the cell. They make every event happen throughout the body, and without them life would immediately cease. Everything we do is the result of enzymatic reactions, whether we walk, talk, blink, twitch, smile, flex muscles, chew, or think.

All voluntary and involuntary actions throughout the body are created through the chain reactions of enzymes. Lifting a finger a fraction of an inch is the result of a complicated sequence of enzymatic reactions. Yet, we relentlessly put substances in our bodies that are dead, their enzymes missing, and expect to get life and health from them. Instead, we get disease, accelerated aging, and early death. This should be no surprise to us. We cannot extract life from dead things. Enzymes essentially *are* the body because they are directly responsible for life itself in a biological sense. Remove the enzymes from any living cell and it will immediately die.

We will never learn to reproduce or synthesize an enzyme because they are catalysts that give off energy in the form of radiation as they react with other enzymes, amino acids or chemical substances. It remains a mystery as to exactly how and why this energy release occurs, but no other phenomenon in the universe parallels the characteristics of enzymes. They are exclusively a work of God that cannot even be imitated, let alone reproduced. Each enzyme is a nano-miracle.

Enzymes are involved in numerous reactions throughout the body before they are finally depleted and must be replaced. New enzymes can only be created by another living entity. With animals and mammals, their organs create enzymes.

We are born with a certain amount of enzymes in our body that will quickly be depleted if we do not continue to replace them by consuming living foods. Enzymes are the bank account of our health, and we must constantly make deposits in the account because the body makes a withdrawal each time it uses enzymes to function. If we do not replace these enzymes, the bank account will become empty, looted of its ability that allows the body to function to its capacity. As our enzyme account becomes chronically depleted, the body struggles at first to function, shutting down organs and entire systems until it finally succumbs. Cooked foods strain the body in every way and deplete our enzyme reserve until the vault is empty and consequently the body is near death, unable to function without enzymes.

We force the body to work many times harder than is required to absorb nutrients from the cooked foods we consume because they are dead and denatured. We strain our enzyme reserves. Other areas of the body become neglected, most importantly our immune system. As we age, we deplete our enzyme reserves until we begin to call upon our metabolic enzymes to help digest the food we consume. The body strains ever harder to absorb nutrients. The digestive tract becomes increasingly clogged because of the absence of crucial digestive enzymes whose presence in the gut helps keep it clean and flowing naturally. We should not put anything in our bodies other than substances that contain pure nutrients (i.e., living foods).

What Food Means to Us

Food brings us together in many ways. People gather socially around food more than anything else. When you decide to honor your temple and start eating more living foods, you sometimes alienate yourself from social gatherings that take place around food, especially during the holidays when families get together to share love, gifts, and food—usually a lot of food. Social events have never been a problem for me because I don't judge what others eat even though I myself am constantly judged. In fact, I never comment on what anyone else is eating unless I'm asked about it and then I diplomatically explain to them why cooked foods don't belong in the body and why living foods do. Many will scoff at your decision to adopt a healthier lifestyle. Some will be curious about your new life. Many people will hear you, and some will listen. Those that only hear you tend to nod politely and then carry on with their lives as though you have offered them directions to a place they have absolutely no wish to ever visit. A few will understand and act upon the revelation of health that has been presented to them.

To those who still insist I eat what they are eating, I explain to them that my health is of great importance to me, much more important than what I put in my mouth that might happen to taste good. If they are persistent and suggest that a little meat, potatoes, or other cooked foods aren't going to hurt me, I explain that I have broken my addiction to cooked foods and I don't want to go back to them because they are not the path to health. I enjoy my health the way they enjoy their food. I explain that there is more to food than only taste. I tell them that my living taste buds have been "reminded" of how good fruits and vegetables are. If they persist, I finally tell them that I intend to honor the temple that God gave me by putting the foods in it that God created Himself, living foods that have not been destroyed by man and his invention called cooking. They usually leave me alone at that point.

Like all true Christians, I am a bit of a maverick. If you are not a maverick somewhere in your life, meaning that you are separate from everyone else, you are not passionate about your Christian faith because to be Christian is to be different from the world. I prefer being different from the world because it is a constant reminder of my faith. I reject social norms because they are the norm. If they fit my Christian lifestyle of pursing health that honors God, then I will accept it. If it does not, such as having chicken, mashed potatoes, and cookies at a church social gathering, I politely say no and only say why if I am asked. Those who live by example speak powerful ideas without ever saying a word.

The first thing we should become aware of concerning cooked foods is that they are an *addiction*, the most widespread addiction in human history. We develop our addiction to cooked foods as infants. Often the first food we consume as humans has been cooked or processed. When we view cooked foods in this light, they begin to reveal their true nature, which is harmful to the body. All addictions are unhealthy. Cooked foods are an addiction because they are detrimental to the body for several reasons. *When we do something strictly for the pleasure of it and we can't stop doing it, that is an addiction.* It is unhealthy because we have lost our control over it. To say that eating living foods is an addiction is a misnomer because the nutrients in them are required by the body in order for it to be healthy; therefore living foods should not be considered an addiction any more than breathing should be because the body requires us to breathe to stay alive.

Many people have told me over the years that Alkaline Ionized Water is addictive because they can't seem to get enough of it. This happens because the small water molecule clusters hydrate the body better than it ever has been before and it is crying out for more! However, this does not constitute an actual *addiction* since hydration is something that is required by the body for it to remain healthy. If anything, these practices should be labeled *healthy addictions*.

The seriousness of this concept concerning cooked-food addiction cannot be understated because it is a declaration that cooked foods prematurely age the body, lead to early death, and are essentially *the cause of all chronic disease*. Once we recognize this about cooked foods, we can begin to treat our addiction to them. None of us want to admit that we are addicted to anything, let alone something such as cooked foods that has been at the core of our lives since we can remember. We are taught that disease is inevitable and who it strikes often appears to be random, sometimes completely nonsensical, such as the person who seems to have a "good diet" and yet contracts Crohn's disease, diabetes, or worse. Or the man in his thirties who dies suddenly on the racquetball court of a heart attack or the young woman who gets breast cancer, both of whom outwardly *appeared* to be healthy. Perhaps they were even vegetarians. A "good diet" to most people means you don't eat a lot of junk food such as red meat, potato chips, cookies, and other packaged snack foods. This notion will increasingly become ridiculous to you as you continue to read the pages of this book.

Start New Healthy Traditions

Replace old cooked food traditions with new ones that lead to true health. The times that we live in have never been more favorable to be a *living foodist*. There is a sea change occurring in our fundamental thinking about health. The medical establishment and the various healthcare systems are draining our resources by chasing cures that simply don't exist in the world of pharmaceuticals, chemicals, radiation, surgery, and other artificial treatments. Increasingly, people are realizing that running to the doctor when they get sick only to be treated for the symptoms of their disease rather than the disease itself is doing nothing for their health. Consequently, minds are beginning to open to the alternatives.

Unfortunately, what is normal and natural is now considered "alternative" and the alternative to what is natural (i.e., medical science) is considered mainstream, normal, and our only hope. Without realizing it, we have allowed the medical establishment, a creation of the secular world, to supplant itself as arbiter of what is healthy and what is the "acceptable" thing to do when you are sick, and that is to see a doctor. What we should be seeking when we are sick is the counsel of God and His infinite wisdom, which is to be found in our own bodies. Yet, for most people, not to see a doctor when they are sick demonstrates a serious lack of judgment if not outright insanity.

Our trust in doctors and their artificiality, bred into us from birth, is waning as our innate trust of nature reemerges. Sometimes you need to ride alone for a while until others see the value of what you are doing and begin to follow you. Without doubt, some eventually will. Many will be inspired by your discipline and healthy appearance. They will respect you for honoring your temple. They will respect you because you have respected your own temple and it has come closer to a reflection of what God has intended us to look like: lean, nimble, and strong.

Once you accept the fact that cooked foods are addictive and that you are an addict, a profound choice will be laid at your feet that you will be forced to confront. You will either move toward the living food lifestyle or you will chose to ignore the truth about health and continue on your path of taste and pleasure at the expense of life's ultimate gift, your health.

The living-food diet is the only diet that leads to true health. The constant promotion and marketing of extracts, concentrates, enzymes, and synthesized hormones for health and rejuvenation only serve to confuse the average person who knows little about health. They hear that everything they have been eating is bad for them, although tasty, satisfying, healthy alternatives are never offered to replace everything they know about food. After you've been told your whole life that chicken soup is good for a cold, it's hard to accept that mom was wrong and that living foods, something completely alien to everything you know, *are right*. The cooked-food lifestyle and the world of medicine that attempts to control the innumerable diseases that result from it is one of utter hopelessness. It is a battle that is lost before it is fought. We must realize that battles are won by doing what is necessary to win, not by doing what we want to do. The best the medical establishment has to offer in most cases of disease is radical surgery, severe and often debilitating therapies, and/or lifelong addictions to pharmaceuticals.

The body that is built from the materials contained in cooked and/or processed foods that are void of enzymes is one that is ready to crumble at any moment. A body built from the nutrients found in living foods will put itself into perfect health and last as long as it was built to last, which is many years longer than we find today in the general population. And the body built entirely on a diet of living foods will not die of disease.

When you are challenged by others, know that you regularly practice true health. Know that you are the one honoring God's sacred vessel, your body, which He wants us to maintain so it is robust and disease-free. When practiced absolutely, the reward is absolute. Without doubt, you will rise to the next level of your life. *That is the fine art of true health.*

The True Revolutionary

> For though we live in the world, we do not wage war as
> the world does. (2 Corinthians 10:3 NIV)

We need to revolt against the way we have been conditioned to eat. We must revolt against our carnal appetites and addictions. We must revolt against the foods we eat because we like the way they taste. We must revolt against anything that makes us unhealthy. We must revolt against anything that does not bring us health. To be a true Christian is to be a revolutionary against the world and its conventions and convoluted ways. Rise up against disease as you would any temptation, for it is succumbing to our temptations that fills us with disease. Only you can defeat it with a change in your diet and lifestyle, not marching with a colored ribbon in empty defiance of a disease and certainly not with pharmaceuticals.

> Please test your servants for ten days: Give us nothing
> but vegetables to eat and water to drink. Then compare
> our appearance with that of the young men who eat the
> royal food, and treat your servants in accordance with

what you see." So he agreed to this and tested them for ten days. At the end of the ten days they looked healthier and better nourished than any of the young men who ate the royal food. So the guard took away their choice food and the wine they were to drink and gave them vegetables instead. (Daniel 1:12–16 NIV)

The story of Daniel is the best illustration we have in the Bible of what kind of diet is best for us. The book of Daniel is a book of prophecy, in which Daniel resists eating the king's food and instead eats only "vegetables and water." After only ten days, they clearly understood what kinds of foods they put in their bodies made a profound difference in their health.

Cooked foods surround us. They are prevalent at every social gathering we attend. They are featured in every restaurant. When we eat cooked foods, we do so for two reasons only: because we like the taste and we are under the mistaken impression that they are good for us. You may say there are other reasons, such as comfort or nostalgia, but they are only variations of taste, for it is taste that comforts us, and it is taste we are nostalgic for. It is the tasty things our mothers fed us when we were young that we are more likely to remember, not the things we didn't like but were forced to eat anyway.

Disease is what awaits all of us who live on a cooked-food diet. Look into any nursing home and see your future, broken, ailing, helpless, diapered, regressed back to infancy where others have to tend to your every need, waiting for death to knock on your door. It is the result of what we commonly call "chronic disease," an event that is completely unknown in nature. Those who have subsisted for many years on the living-food diet will more likely still reside in their own homes and will not require others to care for them. It can be your future too if you choose the living foods path, the path that honors the temple that God has given you.

Only a *living foodist* has the ability to achieve great health, perfect health, the kind of health most people only dream of. If you remain on a cooked-food diet, you will never truly be healthy even though the outward symptoms of disease may not manifest themselves for years to come. Disease *always* resides in the body of the cooked foodist whether the symptoms have surfaced or not.

The biggest myth that has been perpetuated through the centuries and remains well-established to this day is that a diet comprised mostly of cooked foods is healthy. Ninety-nine percent of the population will tell you that some amount of cooked foods is required for us to be healthy, but they are wrong. We're also misinformed that many foods require cooking to release their nutrients. Cooking can in a few instances increase the potency and effectiveness of certain nutrients. However, any gain we may get by increasing the bioavailability of certain nutrients in the food will be more than offset by the destruction of its all-important enzymes and thus its rejuvenative powers. Cooking takes a raw detoxifying, alkalizing, nutritious, rejuvenative food and turns it into mere sustenance, something that will keep you alive a week, a month, perhaps a year.

The Greatest Physician in the World

Physician, heal yourself! (Luke 4:23 NIV)

Physicians are required to make Hippocrates's promise to *"First, do no harm."* However, the medical profession was the third-leading cause of death in the United States in 2002.[20] The first and second causes of death were cancer and cardiovascular disease. Around 106,000 people died from the negative effects of pharmaceuticals;[21] 80,000 people died from infections in hospitals;[22] 20,000 people died from errors made while in the hospital;[23] 12,000 died due to unnecessary surgery;[24] 7,000 died due to medication errors in hospitals.[25] Going to see a doctor can be a dangerous proposition. You are nine thousand times more likely to accidentally be killed by a doctor than by a gun.[26] The solution to not becoming a statistic is making sure we don't have to go to the doctor's office or hospital in the first place. That's what this book is all about.

The human body does not make mistakes because it is God's creation. Even when it is ill and functioning to its full capacity to fight the disease, the body knows what to do with real nutrients from living foods when we provide them to it. If provided with the right materials, the body operates perfectly and the medical establishment instantly becomes obsolete in the treatment of chronic disease. Essentially, we are the architects of our own bodies that God has given us. We sculpt them into the shape that we want it to be by exercising and putting foods in them that are either nutritious or harmful. If we are overweight and have health problems it is because our diet is comprised primarily of cooked foods that often don't satisfy our hunger, which results in overeating.

Adults can have the body they had when they were in their prime, regardless of their actual age. Physical decline is inevitable and starts in your thirties only if you are a cooked foodist. Physical decline only happens to living foodists if they never exercise, and even then the decline will not immediately lead to disease but rather to physical atrophy.

It takes discipline, courage, and faith to move to a living-food diet and begin drinking Alkaline Ionized Water. Health requires regularity. If you want to be healthy, *health must become a habit*. Exercise is another critical part of human health that requires discipline and regularity.

It is not the healthy who needs a doctor, but the sick.
(Mark 2:17 NIV)

To find the best physician in the world you need only to gaze in a mirror. Our own body is the best physician we could ever possibly have. It is more skilled than any vetted doctor. We only need to put the right substances in it so the physician can do its job. However, our physician, our temple-body, cannot emerge without the proper nutrients, those which can only be provided by living foods. The physician becomes a magician and performs what appear to be miracles, but in reality it is the human body, our temple, operating the way it was designed to, which in many ways is nothing less than *miraculous*.

Chapter 5

Our Temple Requires Minerals

Minerals are among the most important nutrients required by the body. They are directly and indirectly involved in every bodily process. Along with amino acids (protein), minerals are the basic building blocks of every cell in the body. Most of the physiological processes of the human body cannot occur without the presence of minerals. RNA/DNA, which are the blueprints to each cell, do not function properly without certain minerals. Amino acids cannot be created then formed into proteins, nor can they be absorbed and used by the body without minerals. The same is true for vitamins. While you may be consuming adequate amounts of vitamins, their effectiveness is diminished without the presence of the specific minerals the body requires. Enzymes will not form or function properly without the minerals they require to do so. Minerals are the keys that allow the engine of our health to start. Without them, bodily processes and functions are greatly diminished.

All minerals are essential, meaning the body is not capable of manufacturing them. Therefore, they must be included in our diet. The body is capable of manufacturing certain vitamins and amino acids. Those that the body cannot manufacture are known as *essential*. For instance, the vitamin B complex can be manufactured by the body; however, vitamin A cannot. Therefore, vitamin A is considered essential and must be consumed either from a food source or supplement form. Phenylalanine is an essential amino acid that can be found in almonds, avocados, and bananas, as well as animal sources. Asparagine (aspartic acid) is nonessential because it can be manufactured, or synthesized, by the body, but not without the proper minerals being present.

Each mineral has a different number of protons and electrons, and a specific frequency or vibration. The frequency of a mineral determines how it will interact with the body and ultimately how the body will use it. Iodine, for instance, has the highest frequency of all the minerals we consume. Minerals are conductors or carriers of electricity and magnetism, both critical to our health. Electrolytes are our most important electrical conductors. They include calcium, magnesium, potassium, and sodium. If we completely lack any one of them, many bodily processes will cease to function and we would soon die.

The size of the minerals consumed is important because it is difficult for the body to assimilate large inorganic minerals. Inorganic means that it is not ionic and does not have a charge because of a lack of electrons. Minerals that are too large also cannot be absorbed and utilized by the body's cells. Chelated minerals were introduced in the 1950s. Chelated means they were combined with amino acids in order to enhance their absorbability. Colloidal minerals, which became prevalent in the 1980s, achieved mixed results because they are too large for the cell to easily assimilate in most cases. Angstrom minerals are between 90 and 98 percent absorbable because of their incredibly small size, as the chart below demonstrates.

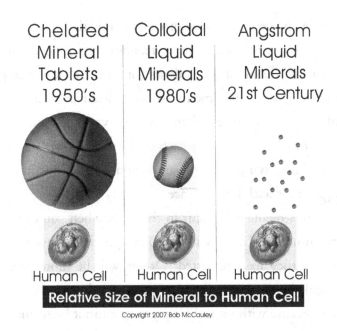

Chelated Mineral Tablets 1950's | Colloidal Liquid Minerals 1980's | Angstrom Liquid Minerals 21st Century

Human Cell | Human Cell | Human Cell

Relative Size of Mineral to Human Cell

Copyright 2007 Bob McCauley

Some minerals compete with one another in the body because they have the same covalence.[27] For instance, copper, zinc, magnesium, and cobalt compete with iron. Fluoride competes with iodine, which is a contributing reason why obesity is so rampant in our society today. Without iodine, the thyroid gland does not function properly and the body's metabolism will not be regulated. Because of the micro-size, angstrom minerals do not compete with each other nearly as much as minerals consumed in other forms. Angstrom minerals are produced in such a way that they are dissolved completely in solution as single minerals that are unattached to any other mineral. When minerals are taken into the body as a complex of minerals that are attached to other minerals, the body does not assimilate them as well as if they are not attached.

Angstrom minerals are extremely effective at detoxifying the body because of their micro size, which allows them to be so absorbable. They easily enter the cell and are able to force out substances that do not belong in the cell, including other minerals that have mistakenly been allowed to enter the cell. Therefore, angstrom minerals encourage a tremendous cleansing of the body and its tissue as it rearranges and makes the necessary adjustments to bring itself back into balance. These adjustments manifest themselves in various ways similar to other detoxification symptoms such as headaches, rashes, diarrhea, and fatigue. These symptoms will subside once your body has cleansed and brought itself back into balance.

Many adjustments will occur in the body when you begin taking angstrom minerals. Most will happen quietly without you ever realizing that they have occurred. Others will be more pronounced and unmistakable. For instance, hair turns gray due to a lack of copper in the diet because without it, hair pigment cannot be formed. When you begin consuming angstrom copper, the body now becomes capable of creating hair pigment and the gray hair slowly disappears.

The only way to be certain which minerals you may be lacking is to be tested for them. A mineral/vitamin/amino acid (MVA) test offers a complete profile of which minerals, vitamins and amino acids you have adequate amounts of and which you do not. It's easy to customize the minerals you are lacking the most if you know your body's needs.

Minerals found in the soil have been significantly depleted over the last fifty years due to runoff and poor farming practices. Because of this, minerals have increasingly become more difficult for us to obtain in our diet, even when a person is consuming a diet comprised of mostly living fruits and vegetables where minerals tend to be more easily absorbed by the body than they are from cooked foods. Therefore, mineral supplementation has become more of a necessity than choice.

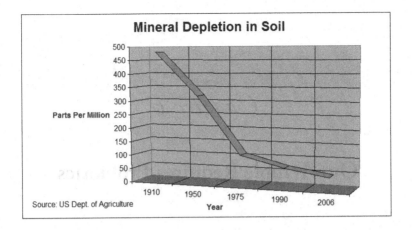

There are no known allergic reactions to any minerals that we consume. If a mineral or metal reacts negatively with the body then it should be considered a toxin and therefore something that does not belong in the body. *(See Appendix II.)*

Chapter 6

Our Temple Requires Probiotics

Probiotics are critical to human health. *Lactobacillus acidophilus* is a friendly bacterium necessary for the digestion of proteins. It also reduces fungus infections, lowers blood cholesterol, aids in general digestion, and enhances nutrient absorption. Deficiencies in probiotics may lead to constipation, bloating, intestinal toxicity, gas, bad breath, *Candida*, mold, and fungal infections.

Probiotics create vitamins in the body. *Bifobacterium bifidium* is key for the synthesis of vitamins K and the B vitamins, including vitamin B12. Deficiency of *Bifobacterium bifidium* can cause constipation, gas, and elevated levels of ammonia from protein digestion, which can lead to liver toxicity. A high level of ammonia in the blood stream decreases appetite and leads to nausea and vomiting. Probiotics are commonly used in the treatment of cirrhosis of the liver and hepatitis. *Bifobacterium bifidium* can be used as a douche to fight yeast infections or as an enema to fight harmful bacteria and improve bowel function, but it should also be taken orally.

There are 2 to 2.5 million different species of bacteria that we have a symbiotic relationship with. We only know what functions a handful of them actually perform in the body. These are known as *probiotics*. At any given time, there ought to be 5 to 6 billion friendly bacterial organisms in our body.

Bad breath does not originate in the mouth but rather the stomach. After eating garlic or onions, a person can have potent-smelling breath, which should not be confused with bad breath. If someone has bad breath, it means the food he or she ate is rotting in the digestive tract and not actually being digested. The quickest and most effective way to stop this putrefaction is with probiotics. When they are constantly present in the body, unhealthy bacteria such as *E. coli, Coliform,* Helicobacter *pylori* (H-*pylori*), as well as viruses, yeast, and mold will not have a chance to culture, thrive, and grow. H-*pylori* is the cause of stomach ulcers, not stress, which many falsely believe. Stress only aggravates stomach ulcers.

Acidophilus and *Bifidobacterium* are used by the body to break food down into absorbable nutrients and keep our digestive tract clean. Probiotics also help the body remain alkaline, a critical key to health. They should be taken before each meal to help us properly prepare for digestion. The probiotics you purchase should be free of dairy products, corn, soy, and preservatives.

When over two hundred senior citizens (ages seventy to ninety) were checked for intestinal flora, over 90 percent were shown to have none in their bodies. This is a shocking statistic since probiotics are critical for human health and should not simply be considered an option. Along with dehydration and fiber deficiency, lack of probiotics is a primary cause of constipation.

Bifidus is essential to our health, and thus we need to keep adequate levels of it in our intestinal tract at all times. Surgery involving the intestines, kidneys, or liver can take a toll on *Bifidus* populations in the body. Antibiotics destroy *Bifidus* and *Acidophilus* in the digestive tract, and thus they should be avoided if at all possible. If antibiotics are used, it becomes even more imperative that we replace our friendly bacteria that are destroyed by antibiotics.

Chapter 7

Our Temple Requires Exercise

> Do you not know that in a race all the runners run, but
> only one gets the prize? Run in such a way as to get the
> prize. (1 Corinthians 9:24 NIV)

Our temple requires conditioning in many ways and for many reasons.
We cannot be truly healthy if we don't exercise on a regular basis.
Having a physically strong, energetic temple is another way we honor
ourselves by honoring God. If you exercise three days a week and not
seven, you are 40 percent of the way to your goal, which should be
to exercise daily. The same is true with regard to moving toward a
living-food diet, as well as the other aspect of this health protocol. Our
goal should be 100 percent for each of them: Alkaline Ionized Water,
spirulina and *chlorella*, probiotics, living foods, exercise, and having
an active, invigorated, profound spiritual life. I get as close as I can to
that every day of my life. This is what is expected from each of us as
Christians. There is no substitute for vigorous exercise, and it is essential
we do it daily if great health is our goal. As with everything concerning
health, consistency is obligatory if you expect to succeed.

It is important that we exercise to the point of perspiring and
deep breathing for a minimum of fifteen to twenty minutes each day

in order to work our cardiovascular system. Sustained diaphoretic breathing invigorates and strains every bodily organ to some degree. Cardiovascular exercise causes oxygen-rich blood to race through our arteries, cleansing everything it comes in contact with. Regular exercise speeds up brain activity and decision-making.[28] It strengthens muscle fibers, joints, and bones.

If you are completely out of shape, the place to begin is walking. Once you get in shape, you can begin to push your limits further until your muscles are strained close to capacity without overtaxing them. With determination, the average person can reach this level of training and exertion in ninety days or less if he or she is consistent in his or her efforts. Always remember that you are training to *your* capacity, to the level *you* are capable of reaching, not anyone else. I am in my fifties and I run six-minute miles at my age because I have trained for years at this level and running comes naturally to me. If your goal is to walk a mile within thirty days because you have an extreme health challenge, then train at *that level.*

There are over 650 muscles in the body, and I make it my goal to exercise each one of them every day, which can be accomplished in as little as ten minutes, although I recommend at least thirty to sixty minutes if you expect to effectively work each muscle. I exercise one to two hours each day between all the various regimens I engage in, which include running, light weightlifting, isometrics, martial arts, pushups, sit-ups, and various other exercises. Rather than give you specific ideas about what kind of exercises you should do, I want only to emphasize that great health is *not* possible without vigorous exercise each day. Exercise builds the immune system in ways that nutrients cannot, which is why it is such an important component if we wish to honor our temple.

It is possible to remain somewhat healthy, meaning disease-free, and not exercise, but without regular exercise, you will never possess robust health, nor will you be able to rid your body of any disease that may be afflicting it. Muscle tissue that is atrophied from lack of use becomes acidic and therefore is more likely to house disease, even for those who consume mostly living foods. Exercise is *that* important.

When we tear down muscle tissue, we then need to rebuild it. We can make it even stronger and more efficient than it was with powerful living whole foods such as *spirulina* and *chlorella* because they include bodybuilding nucleic acids (RNA/DNA) and amino acids (protein), which form the foundation of every cell in the body. I also recommend the *chlorella* growth factor (CGF) for its cellular building and rejuvenative properties. Without these in our diet, building new muscle tissue is substantially more difficult.

Swimming is the best overall exercise for the human body, followed by running. I run four to six miles each day. We can accomplish more physically in the shortest period of time with cardiovascular exercises such as these than we can with any other kind of workout. Combined with upper body and abdomen drills, the entire body is exercised when we use cardio builders such as running and swimming as the foundation of our daily workout regimen. However, if your cardiovascular system is strained by walking because that is all you can manage, then that is the place you need to start. Building up to a power walk and then finally a jog should be your next goals.

Stretching our muscles and conditioning our tendons and ligaments each day is also of great importance to our health. Stretching helps remove blockages and frees up accumulated acid waste throughout the body, especially from the joints and around the organs, even between the cells themselves. Dead cells and other intercellular debris that disrupt critical communication between cells is cleared away by stretching; this is especially effective when it is coupled with daily vigorous exercise. In the body of the living foodist, acid waste is quickly removed, and daily exercise enhances that process. Energy flows more freely through the body when its tissue is flexible, alkaline, and clear of extraneous debris. I spend twenty to thirty minutes each day stretching. Upon waking, it is one of the first things I do because it invigorates the body and mind. Stretching is another critical component of physical health we must practice daily. Healthy habits must become the theme of anyone seeking to be truly healthy. That kind of person is one I call a "*health warrior,*" a person who is forever on the path to better health.

One of the most important benefits of exercise is its effects on the brain.[29] Simply stated, the more we move our bodies, the better our health will be. Even if it's only for a few minutes, it is imperative that we stretch and get *some* kind of exercise each day of our lives if we wish to honor the temple God has given us.

Chapter 8

Our Temple Requires Peacefulness, Spirituality, Religiosity, Meditation, and Prayer

A cheerful heart is good medicine, but a crushed spirit dries up the bones. (Proverbs 17:22 NIV)

Don't you know that you yourselves are God's temple and that God's Spirit dwells in your midst? (1 Corinthians 3:16 NIV)

As God's children, we all possess the gift of self-healing. No food, nutrient, formula, or supplement is capable of healing the body of any disease. Rather, it is what the body does with nutrients that enables it to heal itself of any disease it may have, and only the nutrients found in living foods are suited for this task. Healing is exclusively the prerogative of the body, our temple.

As you begin to move forward in your new life of true health, your trust and confidence in knowing what foods belong in your temple will be nurtured until you are better able to control what you put in your body. Your appetite for foods you know don't belong in your temple will diminish because of how you will feel after you eat them.

There are always more positive things occurring in our lives than we appreciate. Writing them down will allow you to visualize how many you actually have. Monitor your progress toward true health with a chart or calendar. Review your health chart day to day, week to week, month to month. As you move toward what is natural and healthy for your temple, it will reveal nothing but progress toward rejuvenation of the body.

> A cheerful look brings joy to the heart, and good news
> gives health to the bones. (Proverbs 15:30 NIV)

By living to your full potential, you will never have regret in your life. Failure has never scared me nearly as much as the idea of not trying, regardless of what the challenge may be. Regret finds a home in the worthy things we don't pursue. Shame is found in never trying.

> To the pure, all things are pure, but to those who are
> corrupted and do not believe, nothing is pure. In fact,
> both their minds and consciences are corrupted. (Titus
> 1:15 NIV)

The thoughts we have become the reality we create for ourselves. When we live in the moment, we constantly confront ourselves with choices and their consequences, whether immediate or long term. From this we create our own reality, our own path in life, one that either leads toward God or does not. The choice we always face is whether to follow God's way or that of worldliness. We instinctively know which path is just, the right path, the one that leads to God, the best one for each of us. Health is a path we can choose, as is disease. The choice is always ours. None of us were born with the stone of disease and decay tied to our necks. None of us are damned from birth to one day get cancer, diabetes, muscular sclerosis, or any other disease. This is a message meant to wake you from your slumber of complacent, mediocre health. This is a message of self-empowerment, self-determination, and self-reliance. It is articulated so as to free you from the constraints of ignorance regarding how true health is actually achieved.

Daily affirmations and Bible passages are powerful tools that remind us of our goals. Like prayer, they encourage and inspire us. They reaffirm the purpose of our existence and give us an inner confidence that whispers to us that we are doing the right thing, traveling the right path and that God is by our side. They make lifestyle changes such as those I suggest you make in this book easier. They house themselves in our hearts and help us make it through each day with the knowledge of why we do it and the strength to make it a reality.

Anyone can change a single habit, but to dramatically rebuild the foundation of your life is a proposition few of us can manage because it requires dismissing all that we know and deprogramming everything we learned in childhood from those we most trusted—our parents, family, and other role models. But what has been bred into our bones are habits that never allow us to live anywhere close to our potential as they hurry us all to an early demise.

Unless our health has left us and we are in physical ruin, we will never wake one morning and no longer wish to go on if we have a purpose to our lives. People don't want to live to be one hundred years old because nearly everyone they see who is that age is feeble and dilapidated. However, if you wake up on your hundredth birthday feeling energetic, lucid, and pain free, your first thought will be to wonder what your next challenge and accomplishment will be. We will never obtain true purpose without becoming acquainted with our interior selves and having a relationship with God. God must become the purpose of our lives. Part of that must be a constant drive to honor the temple He has given us each day of our lives.

> Then his flesh is renewed like a child's; it is restored as
> in the days of his youth. (Job 33:25 NIV)

Dramatic change in our lives comes easiest when it is done slowly. It has taken me nine years to get to this stage of health, robust and disease free, but I know there is still so much room for improvement. We must approach all things that are greater than ourselves with respect and humility if we expect to learn from them. Only then are we constantly renewed in our purpose, which is to serve God.

The Path We Choose to Travel

> In his heart a man plans his course, but the LORD
> determines his steps. (Proverbs 16:9 NIV)

We must all choose the path our lives will travel. We must make moral choices each day. From time to time, we are confronted with choices that will impact every moment of the rest of our lives. This book was written to present you with such a profound choice.

What will your choice be when it comes to your health? Will you choose to honor your temple and live according to the perfect plan that God has for each of us? Included in His plan are the steps we each take that become the path of our lives. They are the steps we take each day, the strides we take every month and year. Occasionally we take a leap, and if made with faith these leaps we take can sometimes help decide our path in life.

You must become committed to changing the lifestyle that is killing you from within. Change is best begun by a statement, a declaration that from this day forward you will begin to honor the temple that God has given you to the best of your ability, every moment of your life.

If we choose to become a politician, we must dedicate our lives and our daily work to the Lord. If we choose to become a stock broker, we must do the same. No matter the profession, whether skilled, manual, or perfunctory, it is incumbent upon us to do our work for God, not for ourselves, but for His glory, not our own. We must become like the abbot who decided to truly humble himself when his earnest efforts of prayer and fasting had failed and ask for assistance. An act of humility is an act of total surrender to God and His will for us. Deciding to ask for His mercy, forgiveness, and wisdom is the first declaration we must make if we wish to step into His brilliant light and achieve health that is a reflection of God Himself.

> Your faith has healed you. And the woman was healed
> from that moment. (Matthew 9:22 NIV)

If you don't believe it is possible for the body to heal itself of any disease then you need to have faith and know that God does not make mistakes. He does not create faulty designs. If you think gravitating toward this health protocol, God's health protocol, is too difficult, be assured that God will give you strength. God does not give us challenges we cannot overcome. Jesus was able to call Lazarus from the tomb after four days. He will heal you if you place yourself at His mercy and begin putting the right foods in your body. And each morsel of a living food you eat will make you stronger and more resolute in your desire to honor the temple that God has given you.

> Even to your old age and gray hairs I am he, I am he
> who will sustain you. I have made you and I will carry
> you; I will sustain you and I will rescue you. (Isaiah
> 46:4 NIV)

Perhaps you feel it is too austere and drastic a change in your lifestyle I suggest here, that it is too much to ask of you. There would be no possibility of changing the foods and the way you eat, especially at your age. Learning about Christ and following God's way can never come too late in life, and neither can changing your diet so that you can better honor God's temple. The way to begin honoring your temple is to start eating the living foods that you enjoy. Most people should not abruptly stop eating cooked foods and attempt to start eating only raw, living fruits and vegetables. This usually results in disappointment because it is an extremely difficult, although not impossible, life change to make permanent. Move at your own pace, but make sure you are moving in the right direction toward consuming more living foods and less cooked foods, meal to meal, day to day, week to week, and year to year.

When you are saved by learning about Christ and accept Him as your Lord for the first time, you do not immediately stop sinning. Rather, you become aware of your life of sin and how you have been on the wrong path. From that moment forward, sinning becomes less frequent in your life as you truly strive to change your old ways and instead walk with Christ.

Likewise, when you learn the truth about health, you should not expect to change overnight. It will take time, but with wisdom, knowledge, healing and faith your life will change before your own eyes. You will look back on your former lifestyle of deadly habits with great thanks that your eyes were opened and that you had the strength to be disciplined, to endure and prevail over that lifestyle that dishonored your temple and hampered you from living to your potential. It will become one of the great triumphs of your spiritual life.

If you are going to ignore this health protocol, which glorifies the temple that God has given us all, you have placed a wall in front of your spiritual life. If you want to be truly healthy, you must do what nature requires of us. We must try to have a completely clean temple that functions both physically and mentally to its capacity. In this way we truly honor God.

> In your family line there will never be an old man. (1 Samuel 2:32 NIV)

> And the power of the Lord was with Jesus to heal the sick. (Luke 5:17 NIV)

If you are afraid of dying, it is because you have a life worth living. If you are afraid of dishonoring the temple God has given you, it is because you value your spiritual life. Following the way of God is sometimes difficult. Changing your eating habits is extremely difficult, but it will be one of the most rewarding things you will ever do. However, no one can do it for you. You have to do it yourself. Only you can stand in your way of being healthy and experiencing a relationship with God that isn't possible without truly honoring our temple by following the protocol I have outlined in this book.

The best way to begin is to rid your environment of cooked and/or processed foods and surround yourself with living foods. Start with the fruits and vegetables that you enjoy the most and then slowly start trying foods you aren't as familiar with. For example, if you like a spinach salad with tomatoes and onions, that's where you need to start. If you love fruit, then start there. With persistence, one day you'll be sitting in front of foods you never knew existed. In a short time, you very well may be savoring every morsel of it, thanking God for letting it taste so delicious. I had never heard of many of the foods I eat regularly when I changed my diet ten years ago. Now I relish them. I bow my head and thank the Lord that He grew them with such intense flavor and rejuvenative, nutritional, healing properties. In short, I thank Him for the miraculous food He has given to me. I am always humble before a living-food meal, for what I see is God's unchanged creation. Because it is unchanged, it is a powerful yet mysterious thing. We think we understand the properties of God's creations, yet we are unable to create a single living plant or animal. The best science has achieved is the manipulation of God's creation, which we call cloning or genetic modification. When I look at a plate of living foods, I see God's creation. I see the reflection of God. I see a miracle, one that can potentially prevent and even heal the temple of any disease if we only let them work inside us.

The decision you make to honor the temple that God has blessed us with allows us to know Him better, follow Him closer, build and experience a relationship with Him you never imagined was possible.

> Cast off the troubles of your body, for youth and vigor
> are meaningless. (Ecclesiastes 11:10 NIV)

The quality of your health today is more important than the desire for longevity. What good is our life if we are not healthy? As a disease worsens, it makes it increasingly difficult for us to enjoy our life. Youth becomes irrelevant when we are healthy because true health bestows upon us perpetual vitality and juvenescence, that of constantly growing younger and stronger. Grow younger each day with God and know that every step you take is undoubtedly on an endless journey in the right direction. Honoring the temple that God has given us ushers this along in countless ways when we follow God by consuming what is found in nature, which is His creation.

The most important thing in life is your relationship with God. The second is your health. Many will say that the second most important thing in life is family, but what good are you to your family if you are cannot provide for them, if you are a burden to them or if you cannot even spend time with them because you are so sick. Your first obligation to your family is to demonstrate your love for God by having a relationship with Him. Your second obligation is for you to take control of your health.

The other thing that will likely try to stand in your way of obtaining true health is fear. Fear is an acronym for *False Evidence Appearing Real*. Fear is empty. It is puffed up a thousand times bigger than it actually is. It is a thief. Fear steals the precious moments of our lives by making us dwell and squander our energy on it. It makes us stumble when there is no obstacle to stumble on. It makes us want to reach for a light switch when we are standing in the sunlight. Fear is a seed planted in us that will remain dormant unless we make the choice to nurture it.

> Fear knocked on my door. Faith answered it. No one was there.
>
> —Anonymous

Fear is a prerogative of the medical establishment. It operates by intimidating the sick and brainwashing the healthy into believing that disease is inevitable and only artificial treatments and pills that supersede God's creation can save them. It herds us from childhood into their symptom-control industry that never leads to true health. Along with the mainstream media, the medical establishment has convinced us that we do not create an environment within our bodies that invites disease when in fact that is exactly what we do.

Health only can be achieved with support from one another and the help of God. We must not let our doubts betray us. They make us lose the good we might accomplish by breeding fear in our hearts. Fear is nurtured inside the bosom of doubt. It feeds on the absence of God in our lives.

We must not worry, for God feeds the birds. Certainly, He will care for His children. Worry is negative prayer. It is dwelling upon an undetermined result with the idea that its outcome will likely be tragic. Worry invites a negative consequence. It invites negative energy into our lives, the exact opposite of what God is. It encourages a negative result, not a positive attempt at knowing God better.

If we yearn to honor the temple God has given us, we must not fear change, for it is the thing we need the most if we want to succeed. And we must always remember that this profound change in our lives should be done for His sake and His only, not ours. The things we do in the name of God greatly benefit us by doing them.

I wish you the best on your journey to true, natural health by honoring the greatest gift that God has given to each of us—our bodies, which are the temple we share with HimGod.

May God grace you with the strength and determination to follow His path. May He bless you with the gift of great health.

Book Summary

Their fruit will serve for food and their leaves for
healing. (Ezekiel 47:12 NIV)

Jesus speaks of the body as being the living temple of God and refers to
His own body as a temple. His words are misunderstood, as was much
of His message to those who lived in those times. The Bible states that
health and wellness are found with God. If your body is full of disease,
it is because of the choices you have made. All disease comes from our
diet. Our genes have nothing to do with whether we get sick or not.
Disease does not run in our families due to genetics but rather dietary
habits that tend to lead to many of the same diseases.

If we want to be healthy, we must *hydrate, alkalize,* and *detoxify*
(HAD) our bodies, which creates an environment of health within the
body. Alkaline Ionized Water is an antioxidant produced by electrolysis
that Hydrates, Alkalizes, and Detoxifies the body when consumed.
Alkaline Ionized Water is the healthiest substance we can put in the
body because there is nothing better for us than water and there is no
better water than ionized water. The most common cause of disease is
that people don't drink enough water, which leads to chronic cellular
dehydration, where the body's cells are unable to function to their
capacity and serve the body as they are meant to.

Spirulina and *chlorella*, two types of algae, are the healthiest, most
powerful foods on earth. They have the broadest array of nutrients and

are the most nutrient dense of any whole foods. They are 60 percent protein and are what we should use for our protein instead of animal protein (meat, fish, eggs, and dairy). The amino acids (protein) in *spirulina* and *chlorella* are vastly superior to those found in animal protein. They are also high in vitamins, minerals, chlorophyll, and nucleic acids (RNA/DNA).

Living foods (raw, uncooked, unprocessed fruits and vegetables) should be consumed because they also hydrate, alkalize, and detoxify the body. Living foods are filled with enzymes, which only God is capable of creating. Everything we do as humans, whether we think, walk, talk, blink, etc., is the result of enzymatic reactions. Yet we constantly put cooked and processed foods in our bodies that are void of enzymes. The reason we eat cooked foods is because we like their taste and we are under the mistaken impression that they are healthy for us when in fact they are not. Cooked foods should be considered an addiction because they are not healthy for us, yet most of us cannot stop consuming them. It is impractical to believe that we will change our diet overnight to one comprised exclusively of living foods. Instead, we must try to make them as much a part of our diet as possible. We must create new traditions with our friends and family that revolve around living foods that are created by God and have not had their invaluable nutrients destroyed by cooking and/or processing.

Probiotics are the friendly bacteria we require to break down and absorb the nutrients we consume each day. They create vitamins in the body and help keep the digestive tract clean. They also help control harmful bacteria such as E-*coli* and H-*pylori*, which is the cause of stomach ulcers.

Mineral depletion in the soil over the last hundred years has necessitated the use of mineral supplements to compensate for the loss of their availability in our diet. All minerals required by the body are essential, meaning that the body cannot create them, and therefore they must be consumed. Minerals are the keys that start the engine of our health. They give the body conductivity, which is critical for human life. Nearly all bodily processes are dependent upon certain minerals for them to take place. Vitamins and amino acids are unable to be formed and/or utilized by the body without minerals. Angstrom minerals are the most easily absorbed form of minerals because of their incredibly small size.

We must exercise vigorously each day if we expect to be healthy. Exercise builds the body's immune system in ways that nutrients cannot. It helps keep our blood and organs cleansed and well oxygenated.

We also must maintain a positive mental attitude if we wish to be healthy. If we allow negative thoughts to reside within our minds and hearts, all the water and nutrition in the world will not be able to help us. We should strive to have a meaningful relationship with God, which will be greatly enhanced when we honor the temple He has given us, that which we call our body. We do this by consuming Ionized Water, *spirulina* and *chlorella*, living foods, probiotics, and minerals, by exercising, and by having a meaningful spiritual life and a close relationship with God. To accomplish this, we must learn to embrace the sacred principles of wisdom, knowledge, healing, and faith if we expect to truly honor the temple God has given us. This is the path to disease-free living.

Appendix 1

Then the LORD said, "My Spirit will not contend with man forever, for he is mortal; his days will be a hundred and twenty years." (Genesis 6:3 NIV)

People of the Old Testament lived lives much longer than we do today. Perhaps it was their diet, but the Bible is not clear about that. Perhaps it was a steady progression toward a cooked-food diet. The knowledge of how health is actually obtained was forgotten as our taste buds have slowly come to rule our lives. The ravages of succumbing to the whim of what we are accustomed to eating and like the taste of is disease.

- Adam lived 930 years
- Seth lived 912 years
- Enis (Enosh) lived 905 years
- Cainan lived 910 years
- Mahaleleel lived 895 years
- Jared lived 962 years
- Enoch lived 365 years
- Methuselah lived 969 years
- Lamech lived 777 years
- Shem lived 600 years
- Arphaxad lived 438 years
- Salah lived 433 years

- Eber lived 464 years
- Peleg lived 239 years
- Reu lived 239 years
- Serug lived 230 years
- Nabor lived 148 years
- Terah lived 205 years
- Abram lived 175 years
- Isaac lived 180 years
- Jacob lived 146 years

Appendix 2

Essential Minerals and Their Functions in the Body

Minerals are the keys that start the engine of our health.

Bismuth: Digestive problems. Antibacterial. Lyme disease.

Boron: Nervous system. Hormonal balance.

Calcium: Bone health. Nervous system. Regulates blood pressure.

Chromium: Regulates blood sugar and insulin. Weight management.

Cobalt: B vitamin formation. Blood cell formation. Nervous system.

Copper: Premature gray, restores natural hair color. Iron metabolism.

Germanium: Arthritis. Increases oxygen in the body. Digestion.

Gold: Regulates sleep patterns. Brain function. Nucleic acid formation.

Indium: Anti-aging. Maintains hormone function (pituitary and hypothalamus).

Iodine: Thyroid function. Hair, skin, teeth, and nail health.

Iron: Anemia and fatigue. Red blood cell formation. Tissue oxygenation.

Lanthanum: Tooth maintenance.

Lithium: Depression. Regulates serotonin levels.

Magnesium: Heart maintenance. Fatigue. Depression and senility. Bone and tooth maintenance.

Manganese: Adrenal glands and brain. Blood oxygenation. Memory.

Molybdenum: Detoxification. Youthfulness. Anemia.

Palladium: Prostate health.

Platinum: Protects and energizes DNA. Immune and brain function.

Potassium: Heart maintenance. Muscle, brain, and nerve health. High blood pressure.

Selenium: Antioxidant. Immune maintenance. Cadmium and mercury detoxification. Thyroid metabolism.

Silicon: Bodily flexibility. Bone growth. Kidney stones, bladder and liver maintenance. Sleep regulation.

Silver: Antibacterial, antifungal, and antiviral. Lyme disease.

Sodium: Bodily fluid and acid-base balance. HCl production. Cramps. Heat stroke. Nerves.

Sulfur: Skin, nails, hair, liver, and pancreas maintenance. Vitamin and enzyme creation. Reproduction.

Tin: Hair loss. Hearing loss.

Vanadium: Blood sugar. Inhibits cholesterol accumulation. Pancreas maintenance.

Zinc: Wound healing. Digestion and metabolism maintenance. Skin issues. Bad breath. Bone and teeth formation.

Appendix 3

Natural Skin Care

The skin is our temple's largest organ, and it must be cared for daily with great diligence. Each day I exercise vigorously at least twenty to thirty minutes, so I sweat profusely, which cleans my skin pores. Immediately following vigorous exercise I sit inside a far infrared (FIR) sauna for thirty to forty-five minutes. FIR sauna therapy systems duplicate the healthy FIR frequencies produced by the sun. Not only does the perspiration produced by FIR waves contain more toxins and less water, but toxins will also be expelled through the kidneys, liver, and even hair. The increased production of perspiration produces a vast array of healthful benefits. Radiant heat produced by FIR waves is more efficient than conduction heat because it warms the body directly. Conduction heat warms the air that then warms you, which is not nearly as beneficial to us since it only penetrates half an inch into the flesh and does not produce resonant absorption. This inefficient dry heat causes mucous membranes in the nasal passage to quickly dry out, which is why water or steam is often used in traditional saunas. FIR heat alleviates this problem by hydrating these delicate membranes as it clears the sinuses. Sweat produced under normal conditions contains 97 percent water and 3 percent toxins on average. Sweat produced from a FIR sauna is 80 to 85 percent water and 15 to 20 percent toxins. Toxins excreted due to FIR wave penetration include heavy metals, pesticides, and other petroleum-based chemicals, as well as fat itself. None of these toxic substances appear in typical sweat, only in sweat produced from a FIR sauna, in part because FIR waves penetrate so deeply into the flesh.

Weight Loss: Many people who have attempted weight loss through dieting and have not been successful will find a FIR sauna helpful in this regard because often the inability to lose weight is associated with chemical toxicity.[30] As toxins are removed from the body using a FIR sauna, weight loss naturally follows. FIR saunas are the only natural, healthy way to burn calories without exercising.

Cardiovascular Builder: As your body increases sweat production to cool itself, your heart works harder to boost circulation, thus improving your cardiovascular system.[31]

Immune System Builder: As the body's temperature rises to over 100°F, the immune system kicks in to fight the "artificial fever" created by the penetrating FIR waves. This heat also helps detoxify your body by removing the accumulation of potentially carcinogenic chemicals, mercury, and other heavy metals.[32]

Showering

I immediately shower after the FIR sauna so the toxins I have sweated out do not reabsorb into my skin. I use a micro-dermal scrub cloth that is designed to remove imbedded dirt and dead skin cells. I will change the temperature of the water in the shower from hot to extreme cold several times before I get out of the shower. This brings blood to the surface of the skin and invigorates the capillaries as they dilate and contract with the hot and then cold water.

Skin Brushing

After showering, I use a skin brush each day. Skin brushing stimulates the capillaries beneath the skin, which bring blood to it, which helps oxygenate the skin. If you stand in the sunlight and brush your skin you will see an unbelievable sight, that of uncounted flakes of skin flying up into the light. These dead skin cells remain on the skin and add to its aging appearance if they are not removed.

Moisturizers

I use witch hazel and tea tree oil after showering, but I don't use them every day. I don't use oil on my skin since it plugs up the skin pores. If my skin is a little dry in the winter I use shea butter, which is derived from the fruit of the shea tree found in Africa.

Appendix 4

Measuring Body pH

pH is a measurement of the relative concentration of positive and negative ions. When they are present in equal quantities, we have reached a state of equilibrium within the body and our pH will be 7.0. There are two ways to measure body pH, which should not be confused with blood pH. The blood always maintains pH between 7.25 and 7.45. If it falls out of that range, the body will quickly go into shock and death will follow soon after. Anything that does get into the bloodstream outside of that pH is immediately pushed out into the body's tissue.

Body pH

The pH of saliva and urine is a much more accurate measure of overall body pH. I believe that the pH of the body should be approximately 7.0, which is neutral. There are many opinions of what the pH of the body should actually be. I have read as low as 6.3 and as high as 7.2. If you are sick, your body pH will be low. The sicker you are, the lower your pH will be. For instance, if you are a Stage 4 cancer your body, your pH will most likely be near 5.0.

Tools for Measuring pH

Body pH can be measured using pH paper, pH indicator liquid (phenol red), or a digital pH meter.

Measuring with Saliva

The mouth tends to be slightly alkaline, which is why it is a poor barometer of the overall pH of the body. The saliva is a more accurate measure of the body from the waist up, which includes the upper digestive tract. Therefore, it is not a good measure of overall body pH. pH test strips are the only way to test saliva pH.

Measuring with Urine

Many things can affect body pH throughout each day, such as diet and stress level. In order to get an accurate determination of body pH, the urine should be measured first thing in the morning each day for at least week, although a month would be better. As you continue to measure your pH each morning, a profile, or "moving average," will emerge that will be far more accurate than taking a single reading. Urine pH can be measured using pH paper, pH indicator liquid (phenol red) or a digital pH meter.

Glossary

Acid (Acidic): A substance that yields hydrogen ions when dissolved in water. When the body accumulates hydrogen ions, it becomes acid. Any pH below 7.0 is acid. The lower the number, the stronger the acid concentration is.

Acidify: To make any substance more acid by adding hydrogen ions.

Algae (plant plankton): Photosynthetic organisms (eukaryotes), ranging in size from one cell to the giant kelp. Algae were once considered to be plants but are now classified separately because they lack true roots, stems, leaves, and embryos. *See spirulina and chlorella.*

Alkaline: A substance with a pH higher than 7.0. Any substance having properties where there are more hydroxyl ions than hydrogen ions. Anything that is alkaline is considered a base.

Alkalize: To make more alkaline by adding hydroxyl ions.

Antioxidant: Any chemical compound, liquid, or substance that inhibits oxidation. Any substance that contains large amounts of electrons, such as raw foods and Ionized Water, would be considered an antioxidant. The centerpiece of Ionized Water is its antioxidant properties.

Chlorella *sorokiniana* (formally *pyrenoidosa*): A green single-celled micro-algae. Chlorella is the most powerful whole food in the world, which possesses powerful antioxidant, immune-building, and anti-cancer properties. It is renowned for removing heavy metals from the body. There are other strains of *chlorella*, such as *vulgaris*, that are not as powerful or concentrated in nutrients.

Cooked Foods: Any fruit or vegetable that has been exposed to a temperature over 118° F (46° C). Its enzymes are completely destroyed, as is its organic chemical structure. Processed and cooked foods lead to all chronic disease. *See Processed Foods.*

Deionized Water: Purified water that is the exact opposite of Ionized Water. It is water that has been treated to remove minerals. This water should not be consumed.

Detoxification (detoxify): To counteract or destroy any substance that is toxic to the body. To remove toxins, or poisons, from the body. Ionized Water is extremely detoxifying because it effectively removes toxins from the body.

Electrolysis: Changing the chemical structure of any compound through the use of electrical energy.

Electron: The lightest electrically charged subatomic particle in existence. It is one of several small elementary particles that circle the nucleus of an atom. An electron has the same mass and amount of charge as a positron, which is positively charged. Electrons are negatively charged. The average person is starved for electrons.

Enzyme: Any of numerous proteins or conjugated proteins produced by living organisms and functioning as biochemical catalysts. Protein structures produced by the body that cause a chemical reaction. For example, the enzymes produced by the stomach to aid in digestion of food. Metabolic enzymes are responsible for all movement by the body, both voluntary and involuntary.

Free Radical: An atom or group of atoms that has at least one unpaired electron and is therefore unstable and highly reactive. In animal tissues, free radicals can damage cells and are believed to accelerate the progression of cancer, cardiovascular disease, and other diseases.

Fruitarian: Same as vegetarian, but only eats fruit. Some fruitarians will only eat foods that don't kill the plant, such as bananas or apples that can be harvested.

Heavy Metals: There are thirty-five metals that are capable of accumulating in the body and causing serious health problems. Many are commonly found in products often used in businesses and residences. Twenty-three of the metals are quite dangerous: antimony, arsenic, bismuth, cadmium, cerium, chromium, cobalt, copper, gallium, gold, iron, lead, manganese, mercury, nickel, platinum, silver, tellurium, thallium, tin, uranium, vanadium, and zinc. Small amounts of some of these elements are actually necessary for good health. However, large amounts of any of them may cause acute toxicity. Heavy metal toxicity can collect in the sponge-like tissue that composes the brain. They can damage the central nervous system and sap us of energy. They can damage blood cells, as well as the lungs, kidneys, liver, and other organs. Long-term exposure to heavy metals can lead to neuromuscular diseases such as Parkinson's disease, muscular dystrophy, and multiple sclerosis. It can also lead to psychiatric diseases such as Alzheimer's disease and other dementia-related disorders. Most cancer patients who are tested for heavy metals have been shown to have high amounts of them. *Chlorella*, living foods, and the far infrared sauna have been used to effectively help remove them.

Hydrogen Ion: A positively charged species of chemical, symbol H+. The ionized form of the hydrogen atom. Also known as a free radical. The buildup of hydrogen ions in the body leads to accelerated aging and creates an environment for disease to flourish.

Hydroxyl Ion: The anion having one oxygen and one hydrogen atom, denoted as OH-. An oxygen molecule that carries with it an extra electron that can be donated to a free radical.

Ion: An atom or a group of atoms that has acquired a net electric charge by gaining or losing one or more electrons.

Ionize: A process that results in the gain or loss of electrons from an atom. To convert totally or partially into ions.

Ionization: The physical process of converting an atom or molecule into an ion by changing the difference between the number of protons and electrons. The *self-ionization of water* is the chemical reaction in which two water molecules react to produce a hydronium (Acid Ionized Water: H_3O^+) and a hydroxyl ion (Alkaline Ionized Water: OH-).

Ionized Water: Water produced through the process of electrolysis and separated by a membrane into Acid and Alkaline Ionized Water. The alkaline water is an antioxidant; the acid water is for external use only.

Lacto Vegetarian: Vegetarian who also eats dairy products.

Living Food: A raw food. A food that has not been raised above a temperature of 106° F (41° C). Living foods alkalize the body and provide it with rejuvenating nutrients that can reverse its biological age.

Living Foodist or Living Food Vegetarian: Eats only raw algae, fruits, vegetables, nuts, and seeds.

Microwave Oven: Microwaves work on the principle of alternating current. The atoms, molecules, and cells that are exposed to this strong electromagnetic radiation reverse polarity up to 1 billion times per second. Organic matter cannot stand up to this kind of violent energy and completely breaks down. This is known as structural isomerism. This radiation results in destruction and deformation of food molecules and in the formation of new substances (called *radiolytic* compounds) not found in nature. Russian studies on microwaving meat sufficiently to ensure sanitary ingestion caused formation of *d-Nitrosodienthanolamines*, known carcinogens. Microwaving milk and cereal grains converted some of their amino acids into carcinogens. Microwaving human milk intended for breast-feeding chemically alters it, destroying some of its anti-disease properties, such as its antibody *lysozymes* (bacteria-digesting enzymes). Raising the temperature of milk to 150 to 200°F causes it to lose 96 percent of its immunoglobulin-A antibodies.

Mineral Water: Water that contains large amounts of dissolved minerals, such as calcium, sodium, magnesium, and iron.

Naturalist: One who pursues health using the most natural approach, including Alkaline Ionized Water, *spirulina* and *chlorella*, probiotics, raw foods, exercise, and cultivating a positive mental attitude or spiritual life.

ORP (Oxidation Reduction Potential): The ability or potential of any substance to reduce the oxidation of another substance that would be considered an antioxidant. The tendency of chemical substances to acquire electrons from other substances. Also known as redox potential.

Ovo Vegetarian: Vegetarian who also eats eggs. This is the most common form of vegetarianism.

Oxidize: To combine any substance with oxygen, which results in the loss of electrons from that substance. Oxidation of the human body results in accelerated aging. Hydrogen ions oxidize substances, such as those found in Acid Ionized Water. Cooked foods are living foods that have been oxidized. Consuming oxidized substances accelerates the aging process of the body.

Pescetarian: Same as vegetarian, but also consumes fish.

pH (potential of hydrogen): The measurement of the acidity or alkalinity of a solution. A measurement of the electrical resistance between positive and negative ions. A pH of 7 is neutral. Any pH above 7 is alkaline. Any pH below 7 is acid. pH increases or decreases as the concentration of hydrogen ions increases or decreases. The more hydrogen ions, the more acid the solution becomes and the pH decreases. The pH scale ranges from 0 to 14, where 0 is absolute acid.

Probiotics: Live organisms that, when administered orally to establish in the digestive tract, are believed to be favorable to the health of the host. The best-known probiotic is *Lactobacillus acidophilus*. Probiotics counter the decimation of helpful intestinal bacteria by antibiotics. Probiotics given in combination with antibiotics are therefore useful in preventing antibiotic-associated diarrhea. They are a class of "friendly" bacteria that live in the digestive tract where they help to restore and maintain a healthy balance of "good" versus "bad" bacteria.

Processed Foods: Raw foods that have been denatured, robbed of their enzymes and natural chemical structure, and packaged for consumption at a later date. Foods that have been disassembled into their basic chemical components and then reassembled into a synthetic food with a certain texture and taste to make them both palatable and therefore marketable. They have often been injected with either extracted or synthesized vitamins and/or minerals so they can be labeled "Enriched." *See cooked foods.*

Purified Water: The result of removing all minerals from water through the mechanical processes of reverse osmosis, de-ionization, or distillation. It is a pure chemical substance, H_2O. This water should not be consumed.

Redox: Oxidation-reduction. (*See* ORP)

Raw Food (*See* **Living Food**)

Raw Foodist or Raw Fooder. (*See* **Living Foodist**)

***Spirulina* Platensis:** A blue-green algae that is one of the two most powerful whole foods in the world. It is an extremely high-energy food. A microscopic freshwater plant, an aquatic micro-vegetable/organism composed of transparent bubble-thin cells stacked end-to-end, forming a helical spiral filament. *Spirulina* has been consumed for thousands of years. It contains gamma linolenic acid (GLA), well-known for relieving arthritic and rheumatoid conditions.

Spring Water: Water bottled from a source that flows out of the ground. Spring water has a great potential to be contaminated by pollution because it is drawn close to the surface.

Toxin: Any substance that is poisonous to the body. Toxins are things that serve no useful purpose in the human body and therefore should be removed. Alkaline Ionize Water is an excellent way to help remove toxins from the body. All disease lives on toxins.

Temple: A man-made structure where people gather to worship God; the body God has given us.

Trans fat: In the hydrogenation process, vegetable oil is placed under high pressure with hydrogen gas at 250 to 400° F for several hours in the presence of catalysts such as nickel, platinum, aluminum, and other heavy metals that have been implicated in various brain diseases, including bipolar and other dementia-related diseases. This process does not control where the hydrogen atoms are added to the unsaturated double bonds of the fat molecules. Randomly adding hydrogen atoms to polyunsaturated fats converts natural food components into numerous compounds, some that have never been seen until partially hydrogenated fats were invented. This reveals how processing foods changes them into substances that no longer remotely resemble the natural whole foods that are recognized by the body. Trans fats have been scientifically linked to many health problems, including heart disease, diabetes, obesity, atherosclerosis, immune system compromise, reproductive and lactation issues, and cancer.

Vegan: Strictest form of vegetarian. Excludes animal flesh (meat, poultry, fish, and seafood) and animal products (eggs and dairy), and usually excludes wearing or eating any animal products, such as leather, silk, wool, lanolin, and gelatin. Some vegans also disallow bee and yeast products.

Vegetarian: Someone who does not eat meat, dairy, fish, or eggs. Also means *vegan* or *veggie*.

Index

Light of the World

Bob McCauley

About the Author

Bob McCauley, ND (Dr. Bob), is a certified nutritional consultant, certified master herbalist, and owner of the Watershed Wellness Center in Lansing, Michigan. He has published several natural health books, including *Confessions of a Body Builder: Rejuvenating the Body with Spirulina, Chlorella, Raw Foods and* Ionized Water (2000*), Achieving Great Health—the Seven Components of Great Health* (2005), *and The Miraculous Properties of* Ionized Water (2006). Some of his books have been translated into Spanish, including this one.

Dr. Bob is the creator of the HAD method to natural health, hydrate, alkalize, and detoxify your body and inventor of the raw food pyramid and his seven component natural health protocol. Dr. Bob is also the author of *Twelve,* a literary collection of short fiction. He has a line of all-natural health products—many of which were mentioned in this book—called Dr. Bob's Naturals.

Watershed Wellness Center
Lansing, MI 48906 USA
WATERSHED.NET

Dr. Bob's
Raw Food Pyramid

Spirulina & Chlorella
Nuts & Seeds
Herbs & Juicing Grasses
Roots
Sprouts
Fruit
Vegetables
Leafy Greens
ALKALINE IONIZED WATER

Protein
Healthy Fat
Phytonutrients + Antioxidants
Fiber
Medicinal + Healing Foods
Foundation Foods

NatureBuilt

Created by Bob McCauley, ND

Copyright © 2006 - 2015
All Rights Reserved

Positive Mental Attitude

Probiotics

Ionized Water

7 Components of Natural Health

Angstrom Minerals

Vigorous Exercise

Chlorella & Spirulina

Raw Fruits & Vegetables

Copyright © 2012   Bob McCauley, ND

127

Endnotes

1   **Ninth Amendment: Unremunerated Rights.** The enumeration in the Constitution, of certain rights, shall not be construed to deny or disparage others retained by the people.

   Tenth Amendment: Reserved Powers. The powers not delegated to the United States by the Constitution, nor prohibited by it to the States, are reserved to the States respectively, or to the people.

2   **Bodies—the Exhibition.** This phenomenal exhibition has traveled the world educating us on how incredible the human body is. The exhibition displays dozens of human cadavers that have been dissected and then preserved with polymer. This technique reveals the miraculous intricacies and divine design of the body. Literally every inch of both the exterior and interior the body is exposed to the naked eye, including comparisons between healthy tissue and tissue diseased with cancer.

3   "Effects of alkaline Ionized Water on formation & maintenance of osseous tissues," by Rei Takahashi Zhenhua Zhang Yoshinori Itokawa. Study at the Kyoto University Graduate School of Medicine, Dept. of Pathology and Tumor Biology, Fukui Prefectural University.

4   *Secrets of an, Body: The New Science of Colloidal Biology*, by Annie Padden Jubb and David Jubb.

5   Ibid.

6   Judges 20:26; 1 Samuel 7:6; 1 Samuel 31:13; 2 Samuel 1:12; 1 Kings 21:9–16; 1 Kings 21:27; 1 Chronicles 10:12; 2 Chronicles 20:3; Ezra 8:21–23; Nehemiah 1:4; Nehemiah 9:1; Esther 4:3; Esther 4:16; Esther 9:31; Psalm 35:13; Psalm 69:10; Psalm 109:24; Isaiah 58:1–6; Jeremiah 14:12; Jeremiah 36:6–9; Daniel 9:3; Joel 1:14; Joel 2:12–15; Zechariah 7:1–5; Zechariah 8:19; Matthew 4:2; Matthew 6:16–18; Matthew 9:14; Mark 2:18–20; Luke 2:37; Luke 5:33–35; Luke 18:12; Acts 13:2–3; Acts 14:23; Acts 27:9

7   Paracelsus. Swiss-born physician (1493–1541).

8   In 1989, public health officials identified that an epidemic of eosinophilia-myalgia syndrome (EMS), a systemic connective tissue disease, was associated with the ingestion of L-tryptophan taken as a dietary supplement. Fifteen

hundred cases were reported to the Centers for Disease Control and Prevention. At least thirty-eight patients are known to have died.

[9] Forty million tons of methylmercury are released into the environment each year by power plants that burn coal containing mercury. *Mercury in Your Fish*, by Ken Cook, president of the Environmental Working Group.

[10] American Journal of Clinical Nutrition (Vol. 77, No. 2, 504–11) February, 2003.

[11] *Bone mineral density in immigrants from southern China to Denmark. A cross-sectional study.* Wang Q, et al. Eur. J. Endocrinol. 1996 / 134 (2) / 163–67.

[12] "Effect of calcium supplementation on bone mineral accretion in gambian children accustomed to a low-calcium diet." Dibba B, et al. Am J Clin Nutr 2000 / 71 (2) / 544–9., Aspray TJ, et al.

"Low bone mineral content is common but osteoporotic fractures are rare in elderly rural Gambian women," J Bone Miner Res 1996 / 11(7) / 1019–25.

[13] "Examples of diets for infants and children's nutritional guidance, and their effects of adding *Chlorella* and CGF to food schedule," Tokuyasu, M., Tottori City, Japan: Conference proceedings at the nutritional Illness-Counseling Clinic, 1983. Japan Journal Nutrition, 1980, 1983, 41(5), pgs. 275–83.

[14] Dr. Horikoshi did a study in 1979 that showed a significant amount of uranium was removed from people with exposure to this toxin.

[15] *Chlorella, Jewel of the Far East*, by Dr. Bernard Jensen, DO, PhD, 51.

[16] "Vitamin B-12 status of long-term adherents of a strict uncooked vegan diet ("living food diet") is uncompromised." Rauma AL, Torronen R, Hanninen O, Mykkanen H.

[17] "Characterization and bioavailability of vitamin B12-compounds from edible algae." J Nutr Sci Vitaminol (Tokyo). 2002 Oct;48(5):325–31. Watanabe F, Takenaka S, Kittaka-Katsura H, Ebara S, Miyamoto E.

[18] Herbert V. 1994. "Staging vitamin B12 (cobalamin) status in vegetarians." Am. J. Clin. Nutr. 59S:1213S-1222S.

[19] An EFA is any polyunsaturated fatty acid involved in human physiologic processes that is synthesized by plants, but not by the human body and is therefore a dietary requirement.

[20] *To Err Is Human: Building a Safer Health System*. Kohn L, ed., Corrigan J, ed., Donaldson M, ed. Washington, DC: National Academy Press, 1999.

[21] Ibid.

[22] "Incidence of adverse drug reactions in hospitalized patients: a meta-analysis of prospective studies." Lazarou J, Pomeranz BH, Corey PN. Journal of the American Medical Association (JAMA) 1998 Apr 15;279(15):1200–5

[23] Ibid.

[24] "Unnecessary surgery." Leape LL. Annual Review of Public Health. 1992;13:363-83 Department of Health Policy and Management, Harvard School of Public Health, Boston, MA 02115.

[25] "Increase in US medication-error deaths between 1983 and 1993." Phillips DP, Christenfeld N, Glynn LM. Lancet. 1998 Feb 28; 351(9103): 643–4.

[26] Number of physicians in the US = 700,000
Accidental deaths caused directly by physicians per year = 120,000
Accidental deaths per physician = 0.171

Number of gun owners in the US = 80,000,000
Number of accidental gun deaths per year (all age groups) = 1,500
Accidental deaths per gun owner = 0.0000188

To Err Is Human: Building a Safer Health System. Kohn L, ed., Corrigan J, ed., Donaldson M, ed. Washington, DC: National Academy Press, 1999

[27] A chemical link between two atoms in which electrons are shared between them.

[28] Annual Meeting of the Society Of Psychophysiological Research in Montreal, Canada October 18, 2001.

[29] *Spark: The Revolutionary New Science of Exercise and the Brain.* John J. Ratey, Little, Brown and Company, 2008.

[30] "Chemical sensitivity after intoxication at work with solvents: response to sauna therapy," Krop, J., 1998, *J Altern Complementary Med.*, (1)(Spring):77–86.

[31] "Effect of repeated sauna therapy on survival of TO-2 cardiomyopathic hamsters with heart failure," Ikeda, Y. and C. Tei, 2002, *Am J Cardiology*, 90(Aug 1):343–45.

[32] "Mercury exposure evaluations and their correlation with urine mercury excretion: 4. Elimination of mercury by sweating," Lovejoy, H.B., Z.G. Bell, T.R. Vizena, 1973, *J Occup Med.*,15:590–91.

"Chemical sensitivity after intoxication at work with solvents: response to sauna therapy," Krop, J., 1998, *J Altern Complementary Med.*, 4(1)(Spring): 77–86.

"Potential use of the sauna in the long-term treatment of hypertensive cardiovascular circulation disorders—a comparison with kinesiotherapy," Winterfield, H.G, H. Siewert, D. Strangefield, H. Warnke, J. Kruse, U. Engelmann, 1992, *Schweiz Rundsch Med Prax.*, 81(35)(Aug 25):1016–20.

Printed in the United States
by ... distributors.

Printed in the United States
By Bookmasters